ries Editor Scott Miles



# Effective *Reading*



Chris Gough

1

MACMILLAN

Macmillan Education
Between Towns Road, Oxford OX4 3PP
A division of Macmillan Publishers Limited
Companies and representatives throughout the world

ISBN 978-0-230-02914-9



First published 2009



Original design by Designers Collective
Page make-up by Designers Collective; Amanda Easter
Illustrated by Designers Collective; Ed McLachlan; Vicky Woodgate; Amanda Eastwood
Cover design by Designers Collective
Cover illustration/photograph by Designers Collective

**The author and publishers are grateful for permission to include the following copyright material:**
Extracts from *Jane Eyre* (Macmillan Reader) retold by Florence Bell (Macmillan Publishers Limited 1998) copyright © Florence Bell 1998, reprinted by permission of the publisher.
Extracts from *The Last Leaf and Other Stories* (Macmillan Reader) retold by Katherine Mattock (Macmillan Publishers Limited 1999) copyright © Katherine Mattock 1999, reprinted by permission of the publisher.
These materials may contain links for third party websites. We have no control over, and are not responsible for, the contents of such third party websites. Please use care when accessing them.

**The authors and publishers would like to thank the following for permission to reproduce their photographs:**
**Alamy**/Linda Kennedy p68; **AP** pp37, 91, 97; **Brand X** p104; **Corbis**/Ted Levine/zefa p47; **Digital** p78; **Getty Images** pp6, 15, 29, 37, 47, 91, 104(l), 105, Getty Images/Tony Anderson p11, Getty Images/Marco Cristofori p56, Getty Images/Dan Hallman p7; **Jupiter** pp24, 32, 50, 86, 96; **Photographers Choice** pp14, 52(r, l, c), 60, 68(t); **Riser** p42; **Science Photo Library** pp83, 84; **Taxi** pp7, 11.



Printed and bound in Thailand

2013 2012 2011 2010 2009
10 9 8 7 6 5 4 3 2 1

“*The man who reads is the man who leads.*”

American proverb, mid 20th century

# Contents

# 1 New lives

**PRE-READING 1** **You will read a text about a young Spanish man in the USA. What do you think he will say about his new life? Underline one answer.**

1 He came to the USA *to learn English / to meet new people*.

2 He has started listening to *hip-hop / jazz*.

3 He likes watching *American football / baseball*.

4 American people *are friendly /are not very friendly*.

5 He *misses / doesn't miss* Spanish food.

**PRE-READING 2** **Look at the key words in bold in the text and tick the sentences True (T) or False (F).**

***For example:***

| | | T | F |
|---|---|---|---|
| | If you study **journalism**, you want to be a doctor. | ☐ | ☑ |
| 1 | A **course** is a set of lessons at a school or university. | ☐ | ☐ |
| 2 | Your **free time** is the time that you don't work or study. | ☐ | ☐ |
| 3 | If something is **popular**, people like it. | ☐ | ☐ |
| 4 | **Alcohol** refers to drinks like cola and orange juice. | ☐ | ☐ |
| 5 | If people are **aggressive**, you feel safe. | ☐ | ☐ |
| 6 | If something is **exotic**, it is strange and interesting. | ☐ | ☐ |
| 7 | If clothes **fit** you, they are the right size for you. | ☐ | ☐ |

# Xavier – a Spanish student in Chicago

**A** I'm a student at Granada University. I'm in the middle of my studies, and my degree course is **journalism**. To work in the media, it's very important to speak good English. In the future, I hope to travel a lot in my job, and work with people from all over the world.

**B** I'm studying English at a language school in Chicago, a large city in the American Midwest. My **course** finishes in six months, but I want to stay longer. I'd like to stay for another year, but I'll have to find a job.

**C** I'm really enjoying my **free time** here in the USA. Of course, the nightlife in Spain is good, but in Chicago there are fantastic bars and clubs where you can see live music. I've started listening to jazz. In Spain, people don't watch baseball on TV, but here it's very **popular**. I've been to see the Chicago Cubs and the Chicago White Sox play a number of times.

**D** Not everything is good, though. The winters are freezing, and the wind blows right through you. I understand why they call it the 'Windy City'. Most people are very friendly, but I don't feel as safe as I do in Spain, especially at night. Young people drink a lot of **alcohol**, and they can get quite **aggressive**.

**E** You can buy all types of **exotic** food in the shops in Chicago, but it isn't easy to find good *jamón serrano*, a type of Spanish ham. In Granada, I eat it all the time. Whenever family or friends come from Spain to visit me, I ask them to bring some *jamón serrano* with them.

**F** I'm pleased that I have enough clothes with me. American men are generally taller than I am, so it's quite difficult to find trousers in Chicago that **fit** me.

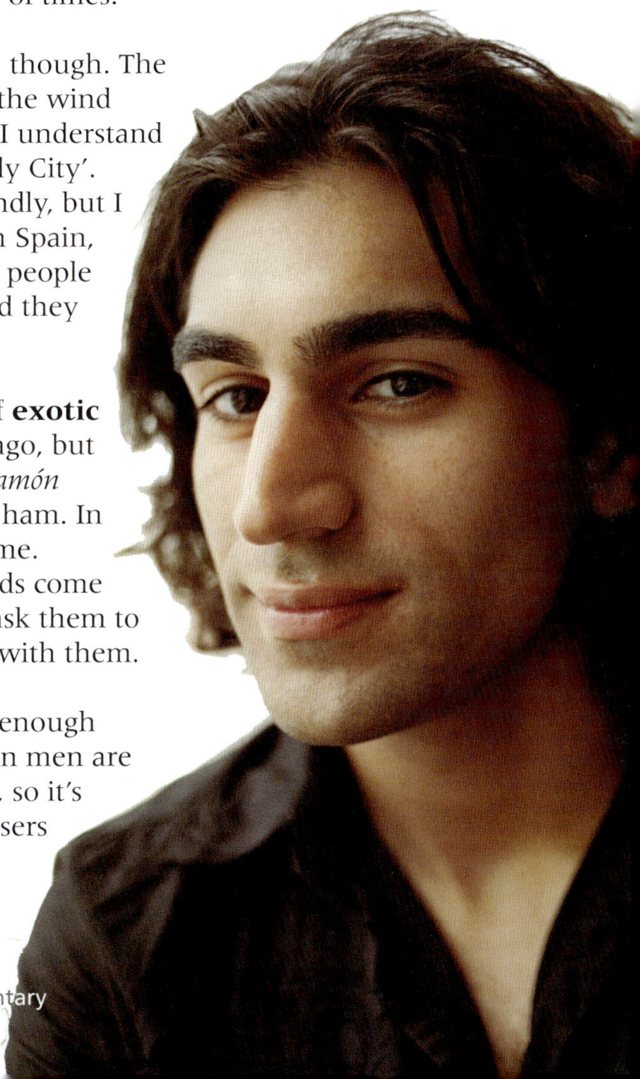

## COMPREHENSION 1 Read the text and match the questions (1–6) to the paragraphs (A–F).

1 Is there anything you are not so happy about? ______

2 What was the most important thing you brought with you from Spain? ______

3 What do you like about life in the USA? ______

4 How long do you plan to stay? ______

5 Why did you come to the USA? ______

6 What do you miss most about Spain? ______

## COMPREHENSION 2 Read the text again and answer the questions.

**1** In line 1, *in the middle* means …

**a** near the start.
**b** near the end.
**c** between the start and the end.

**2** In line 2, *in the media* means …

**a** in television, radio, and newspapers.
**b** teaching a language.
**c** travelling.

**3** In line 10, *enjoying my free time* means …

**a** wanting to have more free time.
**b** not getting much free time.
**c** being happy when I have free time.

**4** In line 11, *fantastic* means …

**a** not very good.
**b** very good.
**c** expensive.

**5** In line 12, *live music* is …

**a** on a CD.
**b** played in the place that you are in.
**c** very good.

**6** In lines 14 and 15, *the Chicago Cubs* and the *Chicago White Sox* are …

**a** places in Chicago.
**b** interesting buildings.
**c** baseball teams.

7 In line 17, *freezing* means …

a very cold.
b quite warm.
c snowy.

8 In lines 17 and 18, *if the wind blows right through you* …

a it is difficult to feel warm.
b you fall down.
c it hurts you badly.

9 In line 29, *have enough clothes* means that he has …

a less than he needs.
b what he needs.
c more than he needs.

## COMPREHENSION 3

### Match the adjectives (1–8) and nouns (a–h) that go together in the text.

*friendly*

*large*

| | |
|---|---|
| 1 good | a bars and clubs |
| 2 large | b people |
| 3 fantastic | c English |
| 4 live | d winter |
| 5 freezing | e food |
| 6 friendly | f young people |
| 7 aggressive | g music |
| 8 exotic | h city |

### These adjectives go with a lot of other nouns. Underline the word that is **not** correct.

***For example:***

| | |
|---|---|
| good | weather / ~~sky~~ / luck / little boy |
| 1 small | man / house / noise / pieces |
| 2 fantastic | weather / holiday / news / pain |
| 3 live | football match / party / concert / interview |
| 4 freezing | light / night / water / hands |
| 5 friendly | holiday / neighbours / dog / smile |
| 6 aggressive | behaviour / chat / argument / attitude |
| 7 exotic | island / drink / animals / news |

**Grammar**
Adjectives and infinitives

If we use a verb clause after an adjective, the verb is an infinitive.
*It's very* ***important to speak*** *good English.*
*It's* ***difficult to find*** *trousers that fit.*

**GRAMMAR 1** Change the sentences using an infinitive after the adjective.

*For example:*

In the USA, finding clothes that fit is difficult.

It's *difficult to find* clothes that fit.

1 Learning English in 6 months is impossible.

It's ______________ English in 6 months.

2 Making friends in a new country isn't easy.

It isn't ______________ friends in a new country.

3 Talking with food in your mouth is rude.

It's ______________ with food in your mouth.

4 Seeing how people live in other countries is interesting.

It's ______________ how people live in other countries.

**GRAMMAR 2** Complete the sentences so they are true for you. Then compare your answers with a partner.

1 I think it's easy to ______________
2 It's difficult for me to ______________
3 I think it's interesting to ______________
4 In my country, it's unusual to ______________
5 In my country, it's impossible to ______________
6 In my country, it's very rude to ______________

**SPEAKING** Talk to a partner and answer the questions.

1 Would you like to live in another country for a year or two?
2 Where would you like to go?
3 Would you miss the same things as Xavier?
4 What else would you miss about your country?

# Effective *Skills*

**PREDICTING** **You will read about Julie, an American woman working as a computer programmer in Spain. Try to guess what she says about living in Spain. Write one word in each space.**

1 She has made some good Spanish ______________.
2 She loves the way people ______________ in the street.
3 People don't mind if there are ______________ in bars.
4 She has bought Spanish ______________ and will send it back to the USA by ship.
5 She doesn't like the noise of small ______________.
6 She misses American ______________.

**SKIMMING AND SCANNING** **Read the text quickly and write Julie's answers (A–F) in the spaces in the text.**

**A** I can travel around easily
**B** I would love to just sit and watch a good show
**C** I'll stay here for the rest of my life
**D** I have photos of my family and my friends
**E** ~~I suppose I'm here~~
**F** find it difficult to sleep well

## *Julie* – a computer programmer in Barcelona

• Why did you come to Spain?
I came to Barcelona because my company offered me a position here. There are lots of Spanish computer programmers but the bosses feel that there should be some American people working here too. _I suppose I'm here_ to learn more about the way they do things in Europe.

• How long do you plan to stay?
When I arrived I planned to stay for a year but that was two years ago. I've made some very good Spanish friends so I have no plans to go home. At the same time, I don't think ________________________________.

• What do you like about life in Spain?
There are lots of things. The food is fantastic and I love the way people eat at tables out in the street. People don't mind if there

are children in bars like they do in some countries. Spain is small compared to the USA and ______________________________ ________. It's very cheap to travel on buses and trains. I adore Spanish furniture. I have bought a table, some chairs and a bed so I will have to send them back by ship if I do go home.

- Is there anything you are not so happy about?

______________________________________, especially at the weekend. I live in a big block of apartments and my apartment is at the front. There's a lot of noise outside at night and I hear neighbours coming home very late. A lot of people ride small motorbikes around the city and that drives me mad.

- What do you miss most about the USA?

My favourite TV programmes, especially on Friday and Saturday nights. ____ __________________________________ and be able to understand every word.

- What was the most important thing you brought with you from the USA?

I'm pleased that ______________________________________. They are very important if I'm ever feeling lonely or homesick.

**READING FOR DETAIL**

**Read again more slowly and underline the correct phrase in each sentence.**

***For example:***

Julie came to Spain *to learn Spanish* / *for her job*.

1 Julie arrived in Spain *a year ago* / *two years ago*.
2 She *knows some* / *doesn't know any* Spanish people.
3 Julie *knows* / *doesn't know* when she is going home.
4 It will be *very easy* / *quite difficult* for Julie to get her furniture back to the USA.
5 Julie *likes* / *doesn't like* the noise of small motorbikes.
6 Julie *has got* / *hasn't got any* photos of her friends and family with her in Spain.

**INFERRING**

**Decide if the sentences are probably true (T) or probably false (F). Underline the part of the text that helps you understand.**

| | | T | F |
|---|---|---|---|
| 1 | Julie is unhappy in Spain. | ☐ | ☐ |
| 2 | Julie likes seeing children in bars. | ☐ | ☐ |
| 3 | In the USA, children go to bed earlier. | ☐ | ☐ |
| 4 | Julie hasn't got a motorbike in Spain. | ☐ | ☐ |
| 5 | Julie doesn't understand Spanish perfectly. | ☐ | ☐ |
| 6 | Julie looks at her photos when she is unhappy. | ☐ | ☐ |

## VOCABULARY IN CONTEXT

**Read again and match the words and phrases from the text (1-6) to the definitions (a-f).**

| | | | |
|---|---|---|---|
| **1** | don't mind | **a** | like something very much |
| **2** | adore | **b** | happy |
| **3** | drives me crazy | **c** | unhappy when you are away from home |
| **4** | pleased | **d** | are not unhappy about |
| **5** | lonely | **e** | makes me very angry |
| **6** | homesick | **f** | unhappy because you are not with other people |

## USING SYNONYMS

**We don't like repeating words so we use words that mean the same (synonyms).**

***For example:***

'I *love* the way people eat …' and 'I *adore* Spanish furniture'

**Complete the sentences with the words in the box.**

| large | clever | gift | easy | escape | attractive |
|---|---|---|---|---|---|

**1** It's a **simple** computer program, and it's very ______________ to use.

**2** My parents live in a **big** house with a ______________ garden.

**3** I got a lot of **presents** for my birthday. My girlfriend bought me a really lovely ______________.

**4** I need to **get away**. If I don't ______________ soon, I'll go mad.

**5** My children are very **intelligent**. My little boy is so ______________ that he can write his name.

**6** There's a very ______________ new student in my class. She's really **beautiful**.

## CORRECTING ERRORS

**Correct eight words that are spelt wrongly in these notes.**

*Julie came to Spain to work with computers. She doesn't no how long she will stay. She likes the peeple, the food and Spanish firniture. She thinks it's very noizy at nite and there are to many small motorbikes. She misses her favrite TV programmes and her frends and family.*

# 2 Big city life

**PRE-READING 1** **Look at the title of the text and the picture. Use a dictionary and check the sentence that has the same meaning as the title.**

**A** Shanghai is growing bigger all the time.

**B** Shanghai is going down into the ground.

**C** Shanghai is getting more expensive.

**Write the past simple and past participle of *sink* in the spaces.**

________________ ________________

**Look at the picture. Underline one option to complete this sentence.**

I think Shanghai is sinking because there are so many *people / big buildings / cars*.

**PRE-READING 2** **Look at the key words in bold in the text and match them to the definitions.**

***For example:***

the process of building something ___*construction*___

**1** very tall buildings ____________

**2** how heavy something is ____________

**3** write down something that has happened ____________

**4** railway that goes under the ground ____________

**5** two materials used for building ____________

**6** people with important positions in an organization ____________

**7** an area of very wet land ____________

# Shanghai is sinking

**Officials** in Shanghai, the second biggest city in China, say they must reduce the **construction** of new high-rise buildings. Over the last ten years about 3,000 new buildings have gone up, and there are plans for 2,000 more. Shanghai is growing faster than any other city in history. It looks good, but now the **weight** of the **concrete** and **steel** is making the city sink. Many parts are sinking more than a centimetre every year.

The tallest building in China is in Shanghai, and a building that will be the tallest in the world is now going up. It seems that planners are forgetting that the area was once a **swamp**. The rock bed is about 300 metres below the surface and the land is very soft. Officials are worried about what will happen to buildings that are already up, and the city's **underground** network, if construction continues. Some of the underground tunnels are already changing shape.

The problem is worst in the busy financial centre, where there are huge **skyscrapers** on what was farmland not long ago. A report says that land there sank nearly four centimetres last year. Land around the tallest building sank nearly six centimetres.

Officials started to **record** changes in 1921, and they believe the city has sunk nearly two metres since then. There are similar problems in Bangkok and Mexico City, and the people of Shanghai need to understand that construction must slow down. The officials hope to show them how bad the problem is. However, with so many buildings already up, it may be too late.

## COMPREHENSION 1 Read the text quickly and tick (✓) the sentences True (T) or False (F).

1 Shanghai became a very big city quite slowly. T ☐ F ☐

2 The buildings in Shanghai are too heavy. T ☐ F ☐

3 Shanghai now has the tallest building in the world. T ☐ F ☐

4 There are problems in Shanghai because the land isn't hard. T ☐ F ☐

5 The construction is good for Shanghai's **underground** network. T ☐ F ☐

6 Some parts of Shanghai are sinking faster than other parts. T ☐ F ☐

7 The problems started in 1921. T ☐ F ☐

8 Shanghai is the only city in the world that is sinking. T ☐ F ☐

## COMPREHENSION 2 Read the text again and answer the questions.

**1** In line 2, *reduce the construction* means …

**a** build more.
**b** build less.
**c** stop building.

**2** In line 2, *high-rise buildings* are …

**a** very tall.
**b** very small.
**c** very old.

**3** In line 4, *more* refers to …

**a** officials.
**b** years.
**c** buildings.

**4** In line 5, *in history* means …

**a** in the world now.
**b** during all time before now.
**c** in the rest of China.

**5** In lines 10 and 11, *the rock bed* is …

**a** rock under the ground.
**b** an area of the city.
**c** a place where people sleep.

**6** In line 11, *below the surface* means …

**a** in the sky.
**b** to the side of.
**c** under the ground.

**7** In line 16, an example of a *busy financial centre* is …

**a** Buckingham Palace.
**b** Wall Street.
**c** Mount Fuji.

**8** In line 23, *slow down* means …

**a** stop.
**b** happen faster.
**c** not happen so fast.

**9** In line 24, *however* is like …

**a** and.
**b** because.
**c** but.

## COMPREHENSION 3 These key words from the text are used in a new context. Underline the correct word or phrase in each sentence.

1 In a football game, the referee and his assistants are *officials / tunnels*.
2 You really should *reduce / record* the number of cigarettes you smoke.
3 I don't want a cake. I really need to watch my *construction / weight*.
4 Knives and forks are usually made of *concrete / steel*.
5 I couldn't see Alice. She was swimming below the *surface / underground* of the water.
6 I can't believe your dog is so big. He's absolutely *soft / huge*.
7 My brother isn't very good with money. In fact, he is having a lot of *financial / construction* problems.
8 My uncle is rich. He wants to buy some *land / swamp* in Spain and build a hotel.
9 When I travel, I *forget / record* everything I do in my diary.
10 You need to *go up / slow down*. You're driving much too fast.

### Grammar
Subject / object pronouns and possessive adjectives

| subject pronoun | object pronoun | possessive adjective |
|---|---|---|
| I | me | my |
| you | you | your |
| he | him | his |
| she | her | her |
| it | it | its |
| we | us | our |
| they | them | their |

## GRAMMAR 1 Underline the correct word. Check your answers in the text.

1 Officials in Shanghai say *they / it* must reduce the construction of new buildings because *it / she* is growing faster than any other city in history.
2 Some of the underground tunnels are changing *their / its* shape.
3 The people of Shanghai need to understand that the construction of new buildings must slow down. The officials hope to show *them / their* how bad the problem is.
4 The land in the financial centre sank 4 centimetres last year; around the tallest building *it / they* sank nearly 6 centimetres.

## GRAMMAR 2 Complete the text with words from the table.

I came to New York City a year ago with (**1**)_______ wife. (**2**)_______ both really love (**3**)_______. New York gives (**4**)_______ everything we need. We have good jobs and there is so much to do. When (**5**)_______ friends come to see (**6**)_______, we take (**7**)_______ to the Statue of Liberty and Times Square and (**8**)_______ say how exciting the city is. There are so many people from so many different countries. I think it's the mix of cultures that gives New York (**9**)_______ character.

## SPEAKING Talk to a partner and answer the questions.

**1** Is your town or city growing quickly?

**2** What are some of the other problems of living in your town or city?

**3** What do you really like about living in your town or city?

# Effective *Skills*

**ACTIVATING THE TOPIC**

**Tick the sentence below that is true for you.**

I live in a big city, and I like it.

I live in a big city, and I don't like it.

I live in the country, and I like it.

I live in the country, but I want to live in a big city.

**Tick the sentences that are true about the city nearest you. Use a dictionary to check the words and phrases in bold.**

1 It's a good place for shopping.
2 Schools are better than in other parts of the country.
3 It has **a long history**.
4 **Pollution** is a problem.
5 There is a lot of **crime**.

**SKIMMING AND SCANNING**

**Read the introduction and put the percentages into the spaces.**

| 75% | 10% | 50% |
|---|---|---|

1 In 1900, ________ of people lived in cities.
2 Now ________ of people live in cities.
3 In 2040, ________ of people will live in cities.

**Quickly read the rest of the text and put the key words into the spaces in the text.**

| shopping | schools | history | pollution | crime |
|---|---|---|---|---|

CITY

## LIFE IN BIG CITIES – THE GOOD AND THE BAD

In 1900, only one in ten people lived in cities. Today half the people in the world live in cities. In 2040, perhaps three out of every four people will live in cities. About 250,000 people move to a city every day. That means that every month, nearly 8 million more people live in cities. We asked some people who live in the biggest cities in the world what they think.

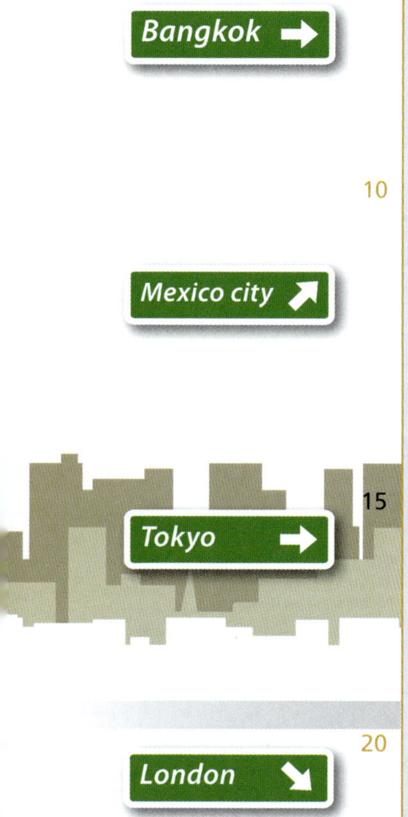


***Jintana from Bangkok***

I love living in Bangkok. It is very cosmopolitan compared to the village where I was born. Everything I want is here. There is music in all the bars, and I can see a different film every night. It can be very noisy, though, and __________ is a problem. There is too much traffic, and sometimes people need to wear a mask when they are walking or riding a bike in the street.

***Manolo from Mexico City***

Mexico City is a fantastic city. It has a long __________, and there are wonderful attractions to visit. The museum is one of the best in the world. There is quite a lot of __________, though, and it can be dangerous. There are parts of the city that you stay away from, especially if you're a tourist.

***Ulrika from Stockholm***

I moved to Stockholm last year, and I love it. I have a better job, and I make more money. There are more bars and nightclubs, and life is much more exciting. I can walk out of my flat and find nice coffee bars and restaurants on my doorstep. The __________ is fantastic too. I can find clothes from all over the world.

***Debbie from London***

I live in London with my husband and two children. Of course, there are some good things about city life, but now that we have children, we want to get away. __________ in London are huge, and there are sometimes 30 or 40 kids in a class.

**READING FOR DETAIL**

**Read again more slowly and write names in the spaces.**

1 Who wants to leave the city? __________
2 Who goes to the cinema a lot? __________
3 Who says that something is very close to his or her home? __________
4 Who says there are too many cars? __________
5 Who says that he or she doesn't go to some parts of the city? __________
6 Who is happier at work than they were? __________

**VOCABULARY IN CONTEXT 1**

**Answer the questions with words or phrases from the text.**

1 In line 6, which word means that Bangkok is a city where you can find things from all over the world? __________
2 In line 9, which word means *cars, lorries, and buses*? __________
3 In line 10, what is something that covers your face? __________

4 In line 10, which informal word means *bicycle*? ______

5 In line 12, which word means *places that people want to visit*? ______

6 In line 14, which phrasal verb (three words) means *don't go to*? ______

7 In line 18, which phrase (three words) does Ulrika use to mean *very near my house*? ______

8 In line 22, which phrasal verb (two words) means *leave*? ______

9 In line 23, which informal word means *children*? ______

## VOCABULARY IN CONTEXT 2

**Jintana calls a bicycle a bike and Debbie calls children *kids*. What do these informal words mean?**

1 I'm going for a drink with a few of my **mates** later. ______

2 I met a nice **bloke** at Sarah's party last night. ______

3 Come over to my **place** for dinner tonight. ______

4 It only costs a couple of **quid** to take the bus into town. ______

5 I always read the **paper** on the bus in the morning. ______

## CORRECTING A SUMMARY

**Change four key words to correct this summary.**

*Jintana says that Bangkok is very cosmopolitan and that there are a lot of bars and clubs. She also says that it's quiet and pollution is a problem. Manolo says that Mexico City has a lot of historical sites, but that some parts of the city can be expensive. Ulrika says that she makes less money working in Stockholm than she did before and that she loves all the restaurants and shops. Debbie says that she wants to leave London because the schools are too small.*

# Review Unit 1

## EXERCISE 1

**Sometimes you need to read quickly and not think about the meaning of every word. Look at the T/F sentences first. Then read the text without a dictionary and complete the exercise as quickly as you can. Write your starting and finishing time.**

Time started: _______

### Marina and Wolfgang - Germans in Spain

Five years ago my husband and I sold our house in Germany and bought a beautiful villa in Spain. We are in our late fifties, and our daughter is grown-up with children of her own. We don't want to work every day. Here we have a lovely garden with a swimming pool and we can enjoy ourselves outside in the sun. We miss seeing our grandchildren every week, but when they come to see us here, they stay for a month and we all have a lovely time.

## EXERCISE 2

**Tick (✔) these sentences True (T) or False (F).**

1 Marina and Wolfgang are now living in Spain.

T ☐ F ☐

2 Marina and Wolfgang are nearly 60.

T ☐ F ☐

3 Marina and Wolfgang have a very young daughter.

T ☐ F ☐

4 Marina and Wolfgang work hard in Spain.

T ☐ F ☐

5 Marina and Wolfgang like the weather in Spain.

T ☐ F ☐

6 Marina and Wolfgang's grandchildren go to see them in Spain.

T ☐ F ☐

Time finished: _______

## EXERCISE 3

**Look at this example from the text.**

*... our daughter is* ***grown-up*** *with children of her own.*

Their daughter has children so she is not very young. She is **grown-up** means that she is an adult.

**Read these short extracts without a dictionary and then underline the correct meaning.**

1 My father lives in Portugal because the **climate** is good for him. All the sunshine makes him feel 10 years younger.

**Climate** means *the type of weather / the type of food.*

2 When I lived in New York, I was always **hard up**. My job didn't pay much and everything was so expensive.

**Hard up** means *very busy / not having much money.*

3 When I was a student in Amsterdam I lived in a **rough** area. I always took a taxi home because I never felt safe walking back.

**Rough** means *there is a lot of crime / it's too far from the centre.*

4 I was really unhappy in Europe. I hated my job and I didn't have many good friends. I decided to **emigrate** to Australia a few years ago.

**Emigrate** means to *go on holiday / go to live in another country.*

# Review Unit 2

## EXERCISE 1

Use your dictionary to check the phrase in **bold** in the text. Then read the text.

### Ever-growing cities

_______________________________. Almost half the people who live in the world's biggest cities are new arrivals, and most of them live in **shanty towns**. In most cities, the conditions in shanty towns are very bad. There is no water or electricity, and there is a lot of disease. The shanty towns are often built on unsafe land and ___________________ _______________.

## EXERCISE 2

Choose the correct first sentence and the correct last sentence in the text.

**first sentence**

**A** The world's biggest cities are the best places to find work

**B** In the poorest parts of the world, cities are growing too quickly

**C** The biggest city in the world is in Brazil

**last sentence**

**A** … are very expensive to live in.

**B** … crime is a big problem.

**C** … can be hit by natural disasters like earthquakes.

Now underline the correct option to summarize the text.

1 The text is *light and informal / formal and serious.*

2 The text is *very positive / very negative* about the situation in the biggest cities.

## EXERCISE 3

Look at the dictionary extracts and then use the words in the sentences.

1 My brother wants to be a __________ like my father, but I want to go to university.

2 The new library is a really beautiful __________.

3 The coast of Spain is very __________ these days. There are a lot of modern hotels and hundreds of bars.

4 If they __________ an airport near my city, it will be much easier to travel.

5 I went on holiday to Greece last year. The hotel was very noisy because there was so much __________ going on in the town.

**build**[1] /bɪld/ (past tense and past participle **built** /bɪlt/) verb ★★★
**1** [I/T] to make a building or other large structure by putting its parts together: *Do you know when this house was built?* ♦ *They're building a new bridge over the river.* ♦ *You need planning permission to build on this land.* **1a.** [T] to make a machine, vehicle, or other structure by putting its parts together: *He's building his own computer.* ♦ *The boat was built to withstand every weather condition.* **1b. be built of sth** to be made from a particular material: *The pyramids are built of solid stone.* **2 build** or **build up** [T] to develop something: *He set out to build a business empire and …*

**build·er** /ˈbɪldər/ noun [C] ★
**1** someone whose job is to build a particular type of vehicle, system, or machine: *a firm of boat builders* ♦ *The software has several new features put in by the builder.* **2** someone whose job is to repair and build houses: *The builders will start work tomorrow.* **3** something that helps to produce or improve something: *a confidence/skills builder*

**build·ing** /ˈbɪldɪŋ/ noun ★★★
**1** [C] a structure made of a strong material such as stone or wood that has a roof and walls, for example a house: *The church is the only ancient building in the city to survive.* ♦ *a group of farm buildings*
**2** [U] the process of building houses, factories, office buildings, etc.: *the building of a new hospital* ♦ *building materials/regulations*

**ˌbuilt-ˈup** adj a built-up area has many buildings in it: *This is the only built-up area on 500 miles of coastline.*

*Extracts taken from the Macmillan English Dictionary*

# 3 A hotel with a difference

**PRE-READING 1** **What is important to you if you stay in a hotel? Check three of the boxes.**

| | | | |
|---|---|---|---|
| The hotel looks nice. | ☐ | The hotel is cheap. | ☐ |
| The rooms are clean. | ☐ | The staff are friendly and helpful. | ☐ |
| The rooms are quiet. | ☐ | It's close to places you want to visit. | ☐ |

**Complete these sentences with one word.**

I think the **Green Magic Tree House** is unusual because it's in the ____________________.

I think the **Ice Hotel** is unusual because it's made of ____________________.

I think **Jules Underwater Lodge** is unusual because it's under the ____________________.

**PRE-READING 2** **Look at the key words in bold in the text and <u>underline</u> the correct definition.**

1 **Guests** are people who *live in India / work in a hotel / stay in a hotel.*

2 A **jungle** is an area with a lot of *trees in a hot country / snow in a cold country / sand in a very dry country.*

3 You use a **ladder** to *climb up and down / sleep in / open a door.*

4 A **bridge** helps you to *move fast / cross from one high place to another / cook.*

5 An **architect** is a person who *lives in a cold country / designs buildings / plays a sport.*

6 **Walls**, **floors**, and **ceilings** are parts of *a car / a building / a country.*

7 A **lodge** is *a part of Florida / a small kitchen / a place to stay.*

8 **Comfortable** means *nice to stay in / not nice to stay in / old.*

# Three unusual hotels

The **Green Magic Tree House**, in India, is the perfect hotel for anybody who likes adventure. **Guests** must drive for miles through the **jungle** to find it in the middle of a tea and coffee plantation.

There are two treehouses to choose from, one 30 metres and the other 35 metres above the ground. Both houses have two floors. The bedrooms are above a living area and there are bathrooms and showers. You can get up to the rooms and move between floors by using **ladders**. You can go from one tree house to the other on a rope **bridge**. The houses sometimes move about in the wind but the views are fantastic.

Guests can enjoy walking through the jungle, climbing in the mountains, and watching wildlife. There are many unusual plants, birds, and insects in the area.

The **Ice Hotel** is in Jukkasjarvi, a village in Sweden 200 kilometres north of the Arctic Circle. Every winter, a team of **architects**, designers and snowbuilders build the hotel. This year there are 80 rooms.

Everything is made of ice, which in this part of the world is crystal clear. The **walls**, the **floors**, the **ceilings**, and even the furniture are all made of ice. The beds are made of ice, too, but guests sleep on warm reindeer skins. Outside it can be -37 degrees centigrade, so inside it feels quite comfortable. The hotel has a bar, where guests can drink vodka from glasses made of ice. It's very popular – because there isn't much else to do.

To spend a night at **Jules Underwater Lodge** in Florida, guests need to scuba dive seven metres under the sea. They enter the **lodge** through a door at the bottom of the building. Inside, the kitchen is stocked with food and there is a fridge and microwave oven. There is a hot shower, and there are **comfortable** beds and lots of books, DVDs, and video games. Most guests, however, spend their time at one of the large windows watching angelfish, snappers, and barracudas swimming by.

## COMPREHENSION 1

**Read the text and tick (✔) the sentences True (T) or False (F).**

1 Green Magic Tree House is easy to get to. T ☐ F ☐

2 Guests sometimes see animals if they stay at Green Magic Tree House. T ☐ F ☐

3 You can visit the Ice Hotel at any time of the year. T ☐ F ☐

4 It is warmer in the Ice Hotel than it is outside. T ☐ F ☐

5 Guests like drinking in the bar of the Ice Hotel. T ☐ F ☐

6 If you want to stay at Jules Underwater Lodge, you need to swim under water. T ☐ F ☐

7 At Jules Underwater Lodge, the only thing to do is watch TV or read a book. T ☐ F ☐

## COMPREHENSION 2 Read the text again and answer the questions.

**1** In line 2, if you *like adventure,* you …

- **a** want to be comfortable.
- **b** you like driving.
- **c** you want to do exciting things.

**2** In line 3, *tea and coffee plantations* are …

- **a** big factories.
- **b** big farms.
- **c** big shops.

**3** In line 8, *rope* tells you …

- **a** what the bridge is made of.
- **b** that the bridge is strong.
- **c** how long the bridge is.

**4** In lines 9 and 10, *the views are fantastic* means …

- **a** you can see everything.
- **b** the treehouses are dangerous.
- **c** the treehouses are very comfortable.

**5** In line 12, *wildlife* means …

- **a** animals.
- **b** trees.
- **c** other guests.

**6** In line 15, *a team of …* means a group of people …

- **a** on holiday together.
- **b** playing a sport together.
- **c** working together.

**7** In lines 18 and 19, *crystal clear* means …

- **a** you can see through it.
- **b** it's cheap.
- **c** it isn't heavy.

8 In line 19, *furniture* is, for example,

**a** walls, floors, and ceilings.
**b** plates, cups, and glasses.
**c** tables and chairs.

9 In line 21, *reindeer skins* …

**a** come from big animals. **b** are beds. **c** are warm lights.

10 In line 28, *stocked with food* means there is …

**a** no food. **b** a lot of food. **c** a little food.

11 In lines 31 and 32, *snappers and barracudas* are …

**a** people who scuba dive.
**b** types of fish.
**c** underwater plants.

## COMPREHENSION 3 Put these words from the text into the correct column.

~~door~~ fish window fridge bird architect wall insect designer bathroom floor microwave oven ceiling reindeer

| parts of a building | kitchen appliances | living things | jobs |
|---|---|---|---|
| *door* | | | |
| | | | |
| | | | |
| | | | |
| | | | |
| | | | |

**Complete the sentences with the words in the box. Use one of the words twice.**

floor fridge wall bathroom ceiling

1 Let's put this wine in the ____________ to keep it cold.
2 In my bedroom, I have a mirror on the ____________ next to the bed.
3 My hands are dirty. I need to go to the ____________.
4 My flat is on the eighth ____________ of a very tall building.
5 There was a big insect on the ____________ right above my head.
6 I'm not a tidy person. I leave my clothes all over the ____________.

**Grammar**

*There is/there are*
*has/have*

We use ***there is*** with singular and uncountable nouns.
***There is*** *a hot shower.*

We use ***there are*** with plural nouns.
***There are*** *two houses to choose from.*

We can use ***has*** and ***have*** to talk about places in a similar way.
*It* ***has*** *a bar, where … Both houses* ***have*** *two floors.*

## GRAMMAR 1 Change these sentences using *has* or *have*.

*For example:*

There is a private bathroom in all the rooms.

All the rooms *have a private bathroom.*

1 There are 80 rooms in the hotel.

The hotel ______________________

2 There is a nightclub on the top floor of the hotel.

The hotel ______________________ on the top floor.

3 There is Internet access in some of the rooms.

Some of the rooms ______________________

## GRAMMAR 2 Change these sentences using *there is* or *there are*.

1 The hotel has a large indoor swimming pool.

______________________ in the hotel.

2 My room has a very good view of the sea.

From my room, ______________________ of the sea.

3 The hotel has five restaurants.

______________________ in the hotel.

## SPEAKING Talk to a partner or in a group of three and answer the questions.

1 Which of the three hotels would you like to stay in? Why?

2 What is the best hotel you have stayed in? Why?

3 What is the worst hotel you have stayed in? Why?

# Effective *Skills*

**ACTIVATING VOCABULARY**

**Look at the picture and the title. Use a dictionary to check the words in bold and check the sentence that you think is true in each pair.**

1 a It is a **luxurious** 5-star hotel.
  b It is a simple 3-star hotel.

2 a The hotel has a lot of single rooms.
  b The hotel has only **suites**.

3 a Guests **check in** at the hotel like any other hotel.
  b Guests can check in at the hotel in their own suite.

**SKIMMING AND SCANNING**

**Read the text quickly and match the ideas (1–5) to the paragraphs (A–E).**

1 what guests can do inside the hotel ____
2 what guests can do outside the hotel ____
3 where the hotel is and what it looks like A
4 what the rooms in the hotel are like ____
5 more about the hotel and why it is different ____

## The best hotel in the world

**A** Many people consider Burj Al Arab Hotel in Dubai to be the best in the world. It is designed to look like the **sail** of a ship, and at 321 metres tall, it is a very impressive building. When it is lit up at night, it is an amazing **sight**.

**B** The 5-star hotel does not have rooms. It has 202 suites, each made up of two floors. Each suite has its own reception desk, so you never need to visit reception. A team of **butlers** provides a 24-hour-a-day service.

**C** Each suite has a luxurious living area, a dining area with a bar, and an office area with a laptop and Internet access. You can operate the plasma screen TV, change the room temperature, or open and close the **curtains** just by touching a button. The floor-to-ceiling windows provide an incredible view of the coast.

**D** Burj Al Arab has eight fantastic restaurants to choose from, and there is a cocktail bar and a cigar lounge. There is a health club, which has two swimming pools, a fitness centre, a squash **court**, a sauna, a Jacuzzi, and massage rooms.

**E** If you leave the hotel, you can lie on the beautiful private beach, play golf, go scuba diving, take a trip in a hot-air **balloon**, or go on a desert safari. If you want to, you can order a Rolls Royce **limousine** with a **chauffeur** to drive you around.

## READING FOR DETAIL

### Read again more slowly and tick (✔) the sentences True (T) or False (F).

1 The hotel looks very good at night. T ☐ F ☐

2 It is easy to make the rooms in the suites warmer or cooler. T ☐ F ☐

3 The windows in the suites are small. T ☐ F ☐

4 You can't smoke anywhere in the hotel. T ☐ F ☐

5 You can do a lot of different sports inside and outside the hotel. T ☐ F ☐

6 You can visit the desert to see animals. T ☐ F ☐

## VOCABULARY IN CONTEXT 1

### Match the words in **bold** in the text to the definitions.

1 a long and very luxurious car ____________

2 a big bag that is filled with air so that it can fly ____________

3 pieces of cloth that you move to cover a window ____________

4 a place where you play ball games like tennis or squash ____________

5 the part of a ship that the wind catches to push it along ____________

6 a person who drives a car for you ____________

7 something that you see ____________

8 people who look after guests in a hotel ____________

*a long and very luxurious car*

**LANGUAGE IN CONTEXT**

**Read these lines again and match the extracts (1–4) to the definitions (a–d).**

**1** **is lit up**, line 3
**2** **by touching a button**, line 11
**3** **take a trip**, line 18
**4** **drive you around**, line 20

**a** go on a journey
**b** take you where you want to go
**c** with a remote control
**d** all the lights are on

**VOCABULARY IN CONTEXT 2**

**Complete the exercise with six positive adjectives from the text.**

*For example:*

b *e s t*

**1** i _ _ _ _ _ _ _ _ _
**2** a _ _ _ _ _ _
**3** l _ _ _ _ _ _ _ _
**4** i _ _ _ _ _ _ _ _ _
**5** f _ _ _ _ _ _ _ _
**6** b _ _ _ _ _ _ _ _

**WRITING A POSTCARD**

**You are staying at the Burj Al Arab Hotel. Complete the postcard to a friend or somebody in your family.**

POST CARD

*Dear __________,*

*I'm in __________ staying at a 5 __________ hotel called the Burj Al Arab. I'm staying in a __________ with my own team of __________ who do everything for me. There is a __________ __________ of the beach and the city.*

*There are a lot of different __________ to do. Yesterday I went on a trip in a hot-air __________ and later today, I'm going on a desert __________. Tomorrow I want to order a __________ and let the chauffeur __________ me around the city.*

*I also really want to ______________________________ while I'm here.*

*Love,*

*__________*

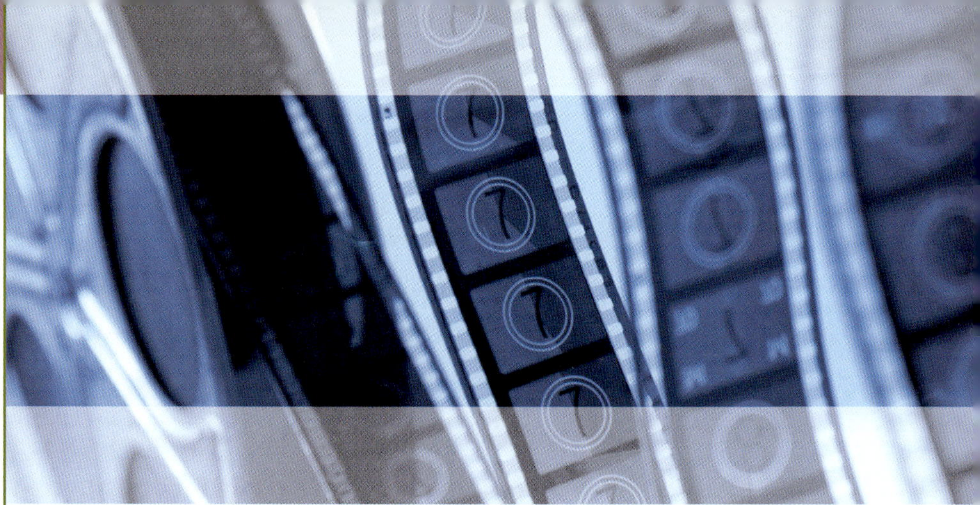

# 4 Making movies

**PRE-READING 1** **Answer these questions.**

1 How often do you go to a cinema to see a film?

2 What kind of films do you like?

3 Which actors and actresses do you like?

**Look at the first two lines from the text you will read.**

Soon, people who go to the cinema will not just watch and listen to the film. They will be able to smell the film, too.

4 Would you like to smell the film when you go to the cinema?

5 Write the names of three of your favourite smells. ___________ ___________ ___________

**PRE-READING 2** **Look at the key words in bold in the text and underline the correct definition.**

1 **Distributes** means *makes / sends to different places.*

2 **Produce** means *make / stop.*

3 **Sense** means *the ability to see or hear, for example / the ability to think clearly.*

4 **Audiences** are *people who travel / people who go to see a film.*

5 **Scenes** are *parts of a film / rooms in a cinema.*

6 **Seats** are *where people sit / people who work in a cinema.*

7 **Liquid** is *water or milk / wood or metal,* for example.

8 If you **scratch** something, *you mark it with something sharp / touch it with your tongue.*

Soon, people who go to the cinema will not just watch and listen to the film. They will be able to smell the film, too. A company that **distributes** films is going to show the world's first fragrant films. A new computerised system, smell-o-vision, will **produce** the smells during *The New World*, a historical drama about the USA in the 17th century. If people enjoy this film, cinemas everywhere may start to use the system.

'Smell is a very important **sense**, and **audiences** will really feel that they are in a market in India or a forest in the Amazon, when they go to see a film,' a spokesperson for the company says.

Seven different smells will be produced during different **scenes** in *The New World*. There will be a smell of flowers during a love scene and a mix of peppermint and rosemary during a very sad scene, for example. Recently, some cinemas produced the smell of chocolate during the children's film *Charlie and the Chocolate Factory*. It was very popular with audiences.

The smells are produced by machines under **seats** at the back of the cinema. Cinema managers will need to pour a fragrant **liquid** into the machines that produce the smells, and because of this, tickets to see a film with smell-o-vision might be a little more expensive.

The idea of smelling a film is not completely new. In the 1970s, cinemas in the USA gave each of the viewers a card as they entered. They could **scratch** the cards with their fingernails during scenes in the film to produce smells.

Smell-o-vision is not just for the cinema. There is a version of the machine that people can use at home or at the office. Smells can be produced to help people relax before they go to bed, or stay awake when they are trying to work.

## COMPREHENSION 1 Read the text and choose the best title. Write it at the top of the text.

The history of world cinema

Smell – our most important sense

Let's go and smell a film!

*The New World* opens soon

Smells can help you relax or stay awake

## COMPREHENSION 2 Complete this summary of the text with one word in each space.

1 The computerised system is called ___________.

2 *The New World* is a ___________ that people will be able to smell.

3 There will be ___________ different smells during *The New World*.

4 ___________ under the seats will produce the smells.

5 There was something similar in the USA in the ___________.

## COMPREHENSION 3 Read the text again and answer the questions.

1 In line 3, *fragrant films* are …

- **a** films you can smell.
- **b** very good films.
- **c** films made with computers.

2 In line 4, *a computerised system* is …

- **a** a lot of computers working together.
- **b** something with different parts that is run by a computer.
- **c** somewhere you can put a computer.

3 In line 5, *a historical drama* is …

- **a** an important thing that happens.
- **b** a kind of film.
- **c** something that happened in the past.

4 In line 10, *a spokesperson* is …

- **a** somebody who talks for other people.
- **b** a manager.
- **c** a worker.

5 In line 13, *peppermint* and *rosemary* are …

- **a** types of flowers.
- **b** scenes in a film.
- **c** nice smells.

6 In line 22, *the viewers* were …

- **a** people who watched a film.
- **b** people who made a film.
- **c** people who worked in the cinema.

7 In line 22, *as they entered* means …

a as they went out.
b as they sat down.
c as they came in.

8 In line 25, *a version of* means …

a a picture of.
b a part of.
c a different form of.

9 In line 27, *stay awake* means …

a not go to sleep.
b sleep well.
c work hard.

## COMPREHENSION 4 Match the senses (1–5) to the body parts (a–e).

| | |
|---|---|
| 1 sight | a nose |
| 2 hearing | b skin |
| 3 smell | c eyes |
| 4 taste | d ears |
| 5 touch | e tongue |

### Now complete the sentences with the correct verb. Use one of the verbs twice.

| see | hear | smell | taste | feel |
|---|---|---|---|---|

1 Can I close the window? I ________ a bit cold.
2 Is the oven still on? I can ________ gas.
3 I can ________ the different spices in this. It's delicious.
4 Did you ________ a knock? I think there's somebody at the door.
5 I can ________ much better with my new glasses.
6 These shoes are beautiful. They ________ so soft.

### Translate this into your own language.

My sister has a sixth sense. ______________________________

**Grammar**

*can/can't*
*could/couldn't*
*will/won't be able to*

*Can* and *can't* express ability in the present.
*a version of the machine that people* ***can*** *use at home*

*Could* and *couldn't* express ability in the past.
*They* ***could*** *scratch the cards during scenes in the film.*

*Will be able* and *won't be able* express ability in the future.
*They* ***will be able to*** *smell the film too.*

*Can* and *could* are followed by the infinitive (without *to*). *Will be able* is followed by a full infinitive (with *to*).

## GRAMMAR 1 Complete the sentences with *can / can't, could / couldn't*, or *will / won't be able* and the correct form of the verb. Some are negative.

1 I ________________ (swim), so I'm taking lessons.

2 When I was a little boy I ________________ (climb) any tree.

3 One day, people ________________ (go) to the moon for their holidays.

4 Cats ________________ (see) in the dark.

5 I'm sorry I ________________ (call) you yesterday. I was busy.

6 In the future we ________________ (buy) petrol so easily.

## GRAMMAR 2 Complete the sentences so they are true for you.

1 I can't ________________, but I can ________________ very well.

2 When I was a little boy / girl, I could ________________.

3 One day I will be able to ________________.

## SPEAKING Talk to a partner. Decide what smells are best for these film scenes.

1 people drinking in a bar

2 children playing

3 a car chase

4 a ship sinking

5 a fight in the street

6 an old house with ghosts

# Effective *Skills*

**ACTIVATING THE TOPIC**

**Look at the picture and answer the questions.**

1 Do you know the actress?
2 Where is she from?
3 Do you know what films she has been in?
4 What are the films about?
5 Which film was important for the actress? Why?

**SKIMMING AND SCANNING**

**Read the text quickly and match the questions (1–5) to the paragraphs (A–E).**

1 What did she want when she was a child? ____
2 What does she think about American films? ____
3 Who is Penélope Cruz? ____
4 Why is she so famous? ____
5 How did she get into the film business? ____

## Penélope Cruz

### Spanish movie queen

A Hollywood beauty Penélope Cruz is one of Spain's best-known stars.

B She really became famous outside Spain in 2001 when she starred in *Vanilla Sky*, a remake of the Spanish film *Abre Los Ojos*. She had a relationship with her co-star, Tom Cruise, but they were only together for three years. She advertises fashion and beauty products, so her face is always in newspapers and magazines. She is regularly included in lists of the most beautiful people in the world.

C Penélope was born in Madrid in 1974. Her father is a businessman and her mother a hairdresser. When Penélope was younger, she wanted to be a dancer, and she studied classical ballet for nine years at one of Spain's best academies.

D People started to notice Penélope when she appeared in a video for a popular Spanish band, and she soon started working in Spanish television. She presented a show for teenagers, and played a part in a popular TV serial. She got her first important film role in1992, when she played *Silvia* in the Spanish comedy *Jamón Jamón*.

E Penélope still enjoys working with directors from her homeland whenever she can, and she doesn't want to live in Hollywood. She thinks that living in Los Angeles could change her personality and that many things about a European lifestyle are preferable.

## UNDERSTANDING DETAIL

**Read again and put the events in Penélope's life into the correct order.**

____ She got a part in *Jamón Jamón*.

____ She went out with Tom Cruise.

____ She starred in *Vanilla Sky*.

_1_ She was born in 1974.

____ She was in a video for a pop group.

____ She learnt ballet.

## INDENTIFYING KEY WORDS

**Underline the correct word or phrase in each sentence and then write the key word in the space.**

1 Pénelope Cruz *was / wasn't* a very important actress in *Vanilla Sky*.

The key word in line 2 is ________________.

2 The idea for *Vanilla Sky was new / came from another film*.

The key word in line 3 is ________________.

3 Pénelope Cruz enjoys working with directors from *Spain / the USA*.

The key word in line 17 is ________________.

4 Pénelope Cruz favours a *European / American lifestyle*.

The key word in line 20 is ________________.

## VOCABULARY IN CONTEXT

**In line 1, *star* is a noun and in line 2, *star* is a verb. Complete the sentences using the words in the box as verbs.**

| book | film | hand | face | milk | water |
|---|---|---|---|---|---|

1. The director wants to ____________ this scene in black and white.
2. I think it's best to ____________ a table before we go to the restaurant.
3. I can't ____________ going to class today, I'm too ill.
4. Farmers get up early in the morning to ____________ the cows.
5. I'm going out to the garden to ____________ the flowers.
6. Could you ____________ me that pencil, please?

## DESCRIBING A FAMOUS PERSON

**Complete this description of an actor or actress that you like. Use the Internet to do your research. Delete any words you don't need.**

______________________________ is an actor / actress from _______

______________________.

He / she first became famous when he / she was in ________________

______________.

He / she also starred in ______________________________ and ______

__________________________.

He / she was born in ______________________________ in ________

______________________.

Before he / she was an actor / actress, he / she was a(n) ____________

__________________.

Now he / she lives in ______________________________.

I really like ______________________________ because he / she _____

__________________________________________________________

__________________________________________________________

__________________________________________________________

# Review Unit 3

## EXERCISE 1

**Look at the verb phrases in Exercise 2. Read the text without a dictionary. Write your starting and finishing time.**

Time started: _______

### Adventure or comfort?

Many young people want adventure when they go travelling. They (**1**)____________________ and find a cheap hostel or guest house when they (**2**)____________________ they are visiting. Older people usually (**3**)____________________ and prefer to arrange their accommodation in advance. For people with small children it is often easier to (**4**)____________________, so that the hotel and all their food and drink are included in the price.

## EXERCISE 2

**Now put these verb phrases in the correct places in the text as quickly as you can.**

arrive in the country
want a little more comfort
buy a package holiday
buy only their flight

Time finished: _______

## EXERCISE 3

**Put the words in the correct order to make typical postcard expressions. Remember to add a full stop.**

1 staying a hotel fantastic I'm at
2 the view window an amazing There's from
3 things are There different do lots to of
4 hotel pool a The huge swimming has
5 a safari going I'm desert on Tomorrow

## EXERCISE 4

**Read these short extracts without a dictionary. Use the context to put the adjectives in bold into the correct column.**

1 The food at the hotel was **delicious**. We didn't need to go out to look for restaurants.
2 The service at the hotel was **awful**. The girls who cleaned the room were so unfriendly, and the waiters didn't know what they were doing.
3 There was a **superb** view from our room. We could see the castle and the snow on the mountains in the distance.
4 The first hotel we stayed in was **dreadful**. The room was really small and the traffic was so loud that it was like sleeping in the street.
5 The bathroom in our hotel was **disgusting**. I don't think anyone had cleaned it for months.
6 The staff at the hotel was **wonderful**. In fact, when we left we bought them a big box of chocolates to say thank you.

| positive | negative |
|---|---|
| | |

# Review Unit 4

## EXERCISE 1

**Read the text without a dictionary.**

### The master of suspense

Anyone who knows anything about films knows that Alfred Hitchcock was one of the greatest directors. His techniques (**1**)____________ the film-making industry as much as any other director. He directed more than 50 thrillers over six (**2**)____________, and became known as 'The master of suspense'. (**3**)____________, his most famous film is 'Psycho'. One of the most famous movie scenes of all time is the scene in which the (**4**)___________female character is murdered in the shower less than half way through the story. Hitchcock had an incredible eye for (**5**) ____________, and the two-minute scene took a week to film.

## EXERCISE 2

**Decide which of these parts of speech go in each space in the text. Write the letter in the space**

**A** noun

**B** verb

**C** adjective

**D** adverb

**Now choose the best option for each space from the list.**

1 discovered / influenced / showed

2 years / centuries / decades

3 Suddenly / Perhaps / Only

4 principal / highest / essential

5 confusion / problems / detail

## 2 IDENTIFYING KEY WORDS

**Read each extract and underline the correct answer in each blue sentence. Then write the key word from the extract into the space.**

1 All my friends said it was a good film, but I really went to see it because the cast looked so good. There are six or seven really famous actors and actresses, and I like them all.

The speaker went see the film because *his friends said it was good / he liked the actors in it*

The key word is ________________.

2 Everything about the film was brilliant. I liked the music so much that I went out and bought the soundtrack. I've played it every day this week.

The speaker bought *a book about the film / a CD of the music in the film.*

The key word is ________________.

3 I saw a film last week, but the plot was very difficult to follow. By the end of the film I was completely lost. I needed to watch it again.

The speaker didn't understand *what the actors and actresses said / what happened in the film.*

The key word is ________________.

# 5 Addicted

**PRE-READING 1** **Check the correct definition for *addicted* in your dictionary.**

**A** You want something very much, but you can't have it.

**B** You do something all the time, and you can't stop it.

**C** You don't like something, so you stop doing it.

**Now look at this question and tick (✔) the boxes *yes* or *no*.**

Do you know anybody who is addicted to …

| | | | |
|---|---|---|---|
| chocolate? | ☐ | coffee? | ☐ |
| shopping? | ☐ | his or her job? | ☐ |
| surfing the Net? | ☐ | cola? | ☐ |
| computer games? | ☐ | football? | ☐ |

**PRE-READING 2** **You will read two newspaper stories about Jenny and Tracy. Jenny is addicted to shopping; Tracey is addicted to cola. Decide if the sentences are from the shopping story (S) or the cola story (L). Use a dictionary to check the key words in bold.**

1 I **spend** about £500 a week. ____

2 I drink 18 **cans** every day. ____

3 It started when I was **on a diet**. ____

4 Waiting for a **parcel** to arrive is very exciting. ____

5 I sometimes **wake up** at night. ____

6 If I can't go out, I do it **online**. ____

7 People tell me it's bad for your **stomach**. ____

8 Sometimes I only **wear** what I buy once. ____

# We just can't stop

**Jenny – the shopaholic**

**A** Since I was a little girl I have always loved shopping. I walked around shops with my mum, begging her to buy me everything I saw.

**B** Last year I finished university and started earning money for the first time. I have a lot of spare cash now, and I spend it all on clothes. I **spend** about £500 a week on clothes, handbags, and shoes. Walking out of a shop with a bag of new clothes is the best feeling in the world.

**C** I need to shop every day. If I can't go out to shop, I shop **online**. Entering my credit card details and waiting for a **parcel** to arrive is very exciting.

**D** Sometimes I only **wear** what I buy once, but I never feel guilty. My dad tells me to stop spending. He says that I've already got a lot more clothes than I need, but I love shopping and I'm not going to stop yet.

**Tracey – the colaholic**

**E** I drink around 18 **cans** of cola every day. If I don't drink it for more than an hour, I feel terrible and I start shaking. It all started 6 years ago when I was **on a diet** and I drank cola instead of eating. After a few weeks, I couldn't live without it.

**F** I have a bottle of cola beside my bed and I sometimes **wake up** at night to drink it. The first thing I do when I open my eyes in the morning is go to the fridge for a can of cola. I always carry a can or two in my handbag. I spend about £300 a month on cola.

**G** I don't know if it's the taste of the caffeine or the sugar, but I know I'm addicted. Friends and people I work with tell me that drinking cola isn't good for you. They say it's bad for your **stomach**, but I like it too much to stop.

**COMPREHENSION 1** **Read the text quickly and match the three pictures to three of the paragraphs. Write the letter of the paragraph in the box.**

☐

☐

☐

### Now write (J) Jenny, (T) Tracey, or (B) both in each space.

**1** Who talks about being a child? ____

**2** Who talks about the cost of being addicted? ____

**3** Who talks about her health? ____

**4** Who talks about what other people think? ____

## COMPREHENSION 2

### Read the text again and answer the questions.

**1** In line 2, when Jenny was *begging*, she means that she was …

- **a** giving her mother something.
- **b** talking quietly.
- **c** asking for something in a strong way.

**2** In line 3, *earning money* means …

- **a** working for money.
- **b** finding money.
- **c** looking for money.

**3** In line 4, *spare cash* means …

- **a** extra money.
- **b** more time.
- **c** more clothes.

**4** In line 9, *entering* means …

- **a** sending something in the post.
- **b** putting words or numbers into a computer.
- **c** trying to open a door.

**5** In line 11, *feel guilty* means …

- **a** to feel bad about something after you do it.
- **b** to feel good about something before you do it.
- **c** to feel good about something while you are doing it.

**6** In line 16, if you *feel terrible*, you …

- **a** feel very good.
- **b** feel very bad.
- **c** feel happy.

7 In line 16, if you are *shaking*, you are …

**a** drinking.
**b** asking for something.
**c** moving without control.

8 In line 20, *open my eyes* means …

**a** wake up.
**b** look carefully.
**c** get out of bed.

9 In line 24, *caffeine* is …

**a** the price of the cola.
**b** the colour of the cola.
**c** an ingredient in the cola.

## COMPREHENSION 3 Complete the sentences with these verbs from the text.

| drink | finish | wear | earn | carry | spend |
|---|---|---|---|---|---|

I've got a good job, so I (**1**)__________ more money than I really need. I'm young, so I don't need to save money. I prefer to (**2**)__________ it on the good things in life. When I (**3**)__________ work, I usually go out for something to eat and a glass of wine. I sometimes (**4**)__________ champagne, which is a bit expensive. I like clothes, too. I (**5**)__________ a suit to work, so I buy a new one every year and I buy new shoes every month. I change my mobile phone every 6 months. I don't want to (**6**)__________ an old-fashioned mobile around.

### Now complete the sentences so they are true for you.

1 If I go out for a drink, I usually have ________________________.
2 At the university, I usually wear ________________________.
3 In my free time, I usually wear ________________________ and ________________________.
4 I spend most of my money on ________________________ and ________________________.
5 I always carry ________________________ with me.

**Grammar**

Present and past simple questions

To form present simple questions we use *do* and *does*. To form past simple questions we use *did*.

The main verb is the base infinitive (without *to*).

*Do*, *does*, and *did* are before the subject. The main verb is after the subject.

| present | | past | |
|---|---|---|---|
| do I | | did I | |
| do you | | did you | |
| does he/she/it | infinitive? | did he/she/it | infinitive? |
| do we | | did we | |
| do they | | did they | |

**GRAMMAR 1** **A reporter (R) is interviewing Tracey (T). Complete the questions.**

***For example:***

R How many cans of cola *do you drink* (drink) every day?

T I drink around 18 cans.

R How _______________ (feel) if you don't drink cola?

T I feel terrible and I start shaking.

R When _______________ (start) drinking cola?

T Six years ago.

R Why _______________ (decide) to start drinking it?

T I was on a diet and I drank it instead of eating.

R _______________ (drink) it at night?

T Yes, I wake up and drink it in bed.

R It must be expensive. How much _______________ (cost)?

T It costs about £300 a month.

**SPEAKING** **Talk to a partner.**

1 One of you is Tracey and the other is the reporter. Practise the interview.

2 Cover the interview and practise again. Try to remember the questions and answers.

3 One of you is a reporter and the other is Jenny, the shopaholic. Ask and answer questions.

# Effective Skills

**ACTIVATING THE TOPIC**

**Look at the picture and answer the questions.**

1 How much exercise do you do every day / every week?

2 Do you swim, go jogging, lift weights or go to aerobics classes?

3 How do you feel if you don't get any exercise for a while?

4 Is it possible to do too much exercise?

**SKIMMING AND SCANNING**

**Read the text quickly and choose the best summary.**

1 Everyone should get some regular exercise.

2 Some types of exercise are more expensive than others.

3 Some people are doing more exercise than is good for them.

4 A lot of models and athletes are addicted to exercise.

## Exercise – the latest addiction

We all know that people can be addicted to drink and cigarettes and that others spend hours texting friends or playing video games. Now it seems that more and more of us are becoming addicted to exercise.

Take Sue, for example. She wakes up three mornings a week at 5.30 to run five miles before going to work. Every evening, she goes to her health club to do aerobics and weight training. Her daily life **revolves around** her exercise schedule. She is a mother, but she spends very little time with her husband or her two young children.

'Exercise addicts are just like any other kind of addict,' says Dr Martin Shaw, from the College of Medicine in Michigan, USA. 'An addiction is something that **interferes with** your job, your social life and your relationships with other people. The addiction becomes the main **focus** in your life and other important things in your life **suffer**.'

Just as people addicted to alcohol need to drink more and more to satisfy their needs, people addicted to exercise need increasing levels of it. The activity that people most **commonly** become addicted to is jogging. Other sports can be expensive. Going to aerobics classes or to a swimming pool costs money, and if you want to lift weights, you need the right **equipment**.

As with most other addictions, an exercise addiction can be an escape from reality, but the media also plays an important part. People see models and **athletes** and want to look the same as them. Consequently, some people think that they are fat when really they are not. Of course, most people know how much exercise is right for them, but an increasing number seem to be **hooked**.

## READING FOR DETAIL

**Read the text again more slowly and tick the sentences True (T) or False (F).**

1 The most important thing in Sue's life is exercise. T ☐ F ☐

2 Dr Shaw says that doing a lot of exercise is good for your job and your social life. T ☐ F ☐

3 People who are addicted to exercise enjoy life more. T ☐ F ☐

4 A lot of people go jogging because it doesn't cost much. T ☐ F ☐

5 Many people who are addicted to something don't enjoy their lives. T ☐ F ☐

6 People who exercise a lot want to work as models or athletes. T ☐ F ☐

## VOCABULARY IN CONTEXT

**Read again and match the words or phrases in bold in the text to the definitions.**

1 things that you need to do an activity ________

2 addicted ________

3 stops something happening in the correct way ________

4 get worse ________

5 is organised around ________

6 people who do sports very well, or as their job ________

7 usually or frequently ________

8 most important thing ________

## UNDERSTANDING REFERENCES

**Underline the noun phrase that each word refers to.**

**1** In line 2, 'others' refers to *people / drink, drugs, and cigarettes.*

**2** In line 16 'it' refers to a *substance / exercise.*

**3** In line 23, 'they' refers to *people / models and athletes.*

**4** In line 24 'them' refers to *their bodies / most people.*

## USING CONJUNCTIONS

**Underline all uses of *and* and *but* in the text. Complete the sentences with *and* or *but*.**

**1** I don't like aerobics, ________ my sister loves it.

**2** My father sold his car ________ bought a running machine.

**3** Children learn very easily, ________ older people are slower.

**4** Too much coffee isn't good for you ________ I drink it every day.

**5** People are lucky if they are clever ________ beautiful.

**6** People are living longer, ________ they will have to work longer, too.

## LINKING IDEAS

**Complete this story with *and* or *but* and some of the words in the box.**

| machines | suffer | turn | equipment | fixed | exercise |
|---|---|---|---|---|---|
| expensive | addicted | revolve | cheap | hurt | |

My father bought a bicycle last month, *and / but* now he's **(1)**________________ to cycling. He rides it to work every day *and / but* then goes for long rides into the country at the weekend. Family life seems to **(2)**________________ around his new bike! He says it's good **(3)**________________ , *and / but* that it takes his mind off work, and / but I think his relationships are beginning to **(4)**________________ . He asked my mother to get a bicycle *and / but* go riding with him, *and / but* she says she's too old for that kind of thing. It's quite an **(5)**________________ hobby, too. He bought all the right **(6)**________________ – shoes, gloves, knee-pads *and / but* a helmet. He even bought a navigation system to put on the front of his bike, *and / but* he got lost on the first day *and / but* he hasn't used it again!

# 6 We love shopping

**PRE-READING 1** **Complete each sentence with *I really like*, *I like*, or *I don't like* so they are true for you. Use a dictionary for the words in bold.**

________________ shopping for clothes and **accessories**.

________________ shopping for shoes and **boots**.

________________ shopping for **jewellery**.

________________ shopping for beauty products and **perfume**.

________________ shopping for CDs, DVDs and computer games.

________________ shopping at **markets**.

**PRE-READING 2** **Look at the key words in bold in the text and underline the correct definition.**

1 If you shop from a **catalogue**, you look at the products *in a shop / in a book*.

2 If something is **fashionable**, it *is very popular / isn't very popular* at a certain time.

3 A **speciality** shop *sells everything / sells a small range of particular products*.

4 If you get a **bargain**, you buy something for *more / less* than it usually costs.

5 A **boutique** is *a big shop with many floors / a small, fashionable shop*.

6 If you go **window-shopping**, you *want to buy windows / look at things in shop windows without buying anything*.

7 A **deli** is a shop that sells *food / books about Mexico*.

8 A **display** is *something that people look at / a Christmas present*.

# Shopping round the world

These days you can look through the pages of a **catalogue**, shop on-line, and buy anything you like on eBay. But nothing can beat actually going out, walking round the shops, and coming home with your shopping bags full. We asked three people to tell us where they love going shopping.

**Samantha, from the USA**

I live to shop, and Paris is a shopper's dream. It offers everything from **fashionable** department stores, full of people buying designer clothes, to local **speciality** shops that are much cheaper.

One of my favourite shops is the Guerlain perfume shop on the Champs-Élysées. I love going there just to look at the beautiful interior of the building. I also love the markets, where you can find fantastic **bargains** if you arrive early in the morning.

When I finish my shopping in Paris in the evening, I go straight to a fantastic French restaurant and order a bottle of the best wine.

**Siobhan, from Ireland**

Shopping in Tokyo isn't cheap, but it's fun. Ginza is an area with a lot of little designer **boutiques**, where you can buy that Armani dress or those Prada shoes that you've always wanted. However, if, like me, you don't have much money, you can just go **window shopping**. There's so much to look at.

My favourite place to shop is the area called Harajuku. It's where the young people of Tokyo can buy all sorts of unusual things. If you want a pair of pink leather boots, for instance, this is the place to go.

**Mike, from Canada**

Shopping in New York City is great, because I know I can buy good-quality products more cheaply there than in London, or Paris. Clothes, handbags, jewellery, books, CDs, and DVDs are all a bit more reasonable if you look around.

I love the **delis**, too. All big cities are very cosmopolitan now, but New York is very special. If I buy a *burrito*, I feel as though I'm in Mexico, and I can even buy fresh coffee beans from a plantation in Jamaica.

The best time to shop in New York, though, is Christmas. The window **displays** are just amazing.

**COMPREHENSION 1** **Read the text and match the three pictures to the three cities in the text. Write the name of the city below each picture.**

1 ________________

2 ________________

3 ________________

**Now tick (✓) the sentences True (T) or False (F).**

1 Samantha likes to go shopping all day in Paris. T ☐ F ☐

2 Siobhan is rich. T ☐ F ☐

3 Mike says that he likes shopping in Mexico. T ☐ F ☐

**COMPREHENSION 2** **Read the text again and answer the questions.**

1 In lines 2 and 3, *nothing can beat actually going out … shopping* means …

- **a** it's better not to go out shopping.
- **b** going out shopping is the best thing.
- **c** shopping from home or going out shopping is the same.

2 In line 6, *I live to shop* means …

- **a** shopping is quite important to me.
- **b** I don't like shopping much.
- **c** shopping is the most important thing to me.

3 In line 6, *Paris is a shopper's dream* means …

- **a** Paris is a very good place for shopping.
- **b** it's easy to fall asleep in Paris.
- **c** Paris is so expensive that people can't really go there.

4 In line 7, *designer* products are products that …

- **a** are cheap.
- **b** have a famous label and are expensive.
- **c** everyone wears.

5 In line 10, *the beautiful interior* means …

- **a** the bottles of perfume.
- **b** the floors, stairs and windows.
- **c** the people who work in the shop.

6 In line 15, *it's fun* means you …

a have to buy a lot of things.
b spend a lot of money.
c really enjoy it.

7 In lines 21 and 22, *a pair of pink leather boots* is an example of something …

a that everyone wears.
b a bit strange.
c typically Japanese.

8 In lines 25 and 26, *are all a bit more reasonable* means they …

a are harder to find.
b are more expensive.
c are cheaper.

9 In line 28, *a burrito* is …

a a Mexican dish.
b a special coffee bean.
c only found in New York.

10 In line 32, *window displays* means the shops have …

a new windows.
b no windows.
c interesting things in the windows.

## COMPREHENSION 3 These key shopping words from the text are used in a new context. Underline the correct word or phrase in each sentence.

1 You smell lovely. Are you wearing that *perfume / jewellery* that you bought yesterday?

2 I like your shirt. Pink is very *fashionable / beautiful* at the moment.

3 I got this jacket for only £10 in the market. What a *display / bargain*!

4 Dubai is a fantastic place to buy *leather / fresh* products like shoes, belts, and handbags.

5 I don't really understand why people like *online shopping / window shopping*. I only enjoy shopping if I buy something.

6 They only charge £1 for a coffee. I think that's very *reasonable / good quality*.

7 Corned beef is a *boutique / speciality* in many New York delis.

8 Marco loves wearing *designer / boutique* sunglasses. He likes people to know how rich he is.

**Grammar**
Articles

We don't use an article with …
general plurals *( … I can buy fresh coffee beans )*
general uncountable nouns *( jewellery isn't expensive )*
countries and cities *( … in Mexico / … in Paris )*

We use *a* and *an* …
when there are many of something, but we talk about only one of them *( … in **a** fantastic French restaurant ) ( Ginza is **an** area with … )*

We use *the* when …
there is only one of something *( … **the** Guerlain perfume store … )*
we talk about a particular plural *( … I also like **the** markets )*
with superlatives *( … **the** best French wine )*

## GRAMMAR 1 Complete the texts with *a*, *an*, *the*, or nothing. Remember to use capital letters, if necessary.

1 I love shopping in ____ Barcelona. There is ____ fantastic chocolate shop in ____ centre of ____ city. ____ chocolates that they sell there are really delicious.

2 Harrods, in ____ London, is probably ____ most famous store in ____ world. ____ people from every country go there to buy ____ unusual things. They say that you can buy anything from ____ sports car to ____ elephant.

3 I go to France every year to buy ____ champagne. While I'm there I love shopping for ____ cheese, too.

4 Akihabara is ____ best place in ____ Tokyo to buy ____ electrical products. ____ shops there are ten stories high and you can buy ____ most amazing mobile phones.

## SPEAKING Talk to a partner or in a group of three and answer the questions.

1 Which of the three cities in the text would you like to go shopping in?

2 Are there any other cities where you like to shop?

3 Why do you like it so much?

4 What do you buy when you go there?

# Effective *Skills*

**ACTIVATING THE TOPIC**

**Complete the sentences about shopping in markets in your country.**

1 A famous market in my country is called ______________________________ ______________________.

2 Most people go there to buy ____________________________________________ _________.

**ACTIVATING VOCABULARY**

**Choose A, B, or C to complete the sentences about markets in your country. Use a dictionary to check the words in bold.**

1 People go shopping in markets because …

- **a** prices are lower than in shops.
- **b** there is a good **atmosphere**.
- **c** the products are better than in shops.

2 Shoppers at markets …

- **a** must pay the asking price.
- **b** can **bargain**.
- **c** get things free.

3 The best **stalls** are the ones where you can buy …

- **a** clothes and **leather** products.
- **b** things for the house.
- **c** food.

**SKIMMING AND SCANNING**

**Read the text quickly, and choose the best title. Write it at the top of the text.**

The largest square in Africa

Marrakech – a shopping experience

How to choose the best leather products

The long history of markets in Morocco

Try a spicy snack in Marrakech

A Forget London, Paris and Milan. The latest place for fashionable Europeans to spend a weekend shopping is Marrakech. With cheap airlines now flying regularly from several airports to Morocco's second-largest city, it has become a very popular destination.

B There are some fantastic hotels, and the weather is warm all year round, but it's the shopping that is now the real attraction. The *souk* is a labyrinth of narrow streets where shoppers can buy almost anything they want. The leather jackets, shoes and belts are very popular, and people love the beautiful rugs and the colourful plates and vases. In the workshops, visitors can see the products being made.

C To get to the *souk*, everyone must pass through the main square, *Djemaa el Fna*, where the atmosphere is strange and exotic. It is the largest square in Africa, and a sea of colour and fantastic smells. Shoppers can stop to watch acrobats and story-tellers, see snakes dancing to the sound of a flute, and watch monkeys running around the outdoor stalls. Many of the stalls sell food, and visitors can stop for a deliciously spicy snack.

D Remember that you should try to bargain when you shop in Morocco. Offer about half of what you want to pay, and take your time about getting the right price. Be ready to walk away if you think the price is too high. The stall-holder will probably call you back to continue bargaining.

E Whatever you decide to buy in Marrakech, you can be sure you will have a weekend to remember, and the souvenirs you bring home will certainly not cost you a fortune.

**READING FOR DETAIL 1**

**Write the paragraph number in the space.**

In which paragraph do you learn …

**1** that you don't always have to pay a fixed price? ________

**2** that it is easier to get to Morocco than it used to be? ________

**3** that the things you buy won't be expensive? ________

**4** that there are unusual things to see while you are shopping? ________

**5** which products are most popular? ________

## READING FOR DETAIL 2

### Underline the correct word or phrase in each sentence.

1 There *is one city / are a few cities* bigger than Marrakech in Morocco.

2 People go to Morocco mostly for *the weather / the shopping*.

3 There are *only a few / a lot of streets* in the *souk*.

4 The main square is *near the sea / full of colour*.

5 People *often / never* eat when they are shopping in Marrakech.

6 Shoppers often pay *more / less* than the asking price in the *souk*.

7 You should walk away from a stall if you *like the product / are not happy with the price*.

## VOCABULARY IN CONTEXT

### Complete the sentences with the key nouns from the text.

1 In the first paragraph, a company that has planes and sells flights is an __________.

2 In the second paragraph, a place with a lot of little streets where you can easily get lost is a __________.

3 In the third paragraph, something small and quick to eat is a __________.

4 In the final paragraph, something you buy to help you remember your holiday is a __________.

### Now answer the questions.

5 Which one of these don't you wear? Delete it.
jackets / shoes / belts / rugs

6 Which of these is not a person or an animal? Delete it.
acrobat / story-teller / snake / flute / monkey

## CORRECTING ERRORS

### Look at these notes about the text. The teacher has highlighted twelve errors. Write the notes again.

- *In Marrakech, ______ city in Morocco, there is the fantastic souk. People go there to shop, enjoy ______ atmosphere and to eat the good foods.*
- *Tourists come especially for a shopping. They can buy the leather products and lovely rug ______.*
- *A main square is ______ biggest in Africa. People can see the snakes dancing to musics.*

# Review Unit 5

## EXERCISE 1

**Look at the sentences below first. Then read the text without a dictionary and complete the exercise as quickly as you can. Write your starting and finishing time.**

Time started: _______

### The habit of a lifetime

I had my first cigarette when I was 16 and I'm still a smoker 25 years later. I've tried to stop a thousand times. When I got my first job, I stopped for two weeks. When I was pregnant with my daughter I gave up smoking, but the week after she was born, I started again. I pretend that smoking reduces stress and that I do it to keep my weight down. Really, though, I know that for me, giving up smoking will be a lifelong battle.

## EXERCISE 2

**Underline the correct option in each sentence.**

1 The speaker is now *25 / 41* years old.

2 She has tried to stop smoking *many times / exactly a thousand times.*

3 She *started / stopped* smoking when she was expecting a baby.

4 She *really believes / doesn't really believe* that smoking reduces stress.

5 She tries to believe that smoking makes her *fatter / thinner.*

6 She thinks that in the future it will be *very difficult / quite easy* for her to stop.

Time finished: _______

## EXERCISE 3

**Complete the sentences with the words. Use each word only once.**

| they | one | them | it | there |
|---|---|---|---|---|

1 My brother thinks about nothing but football. He talks about __________ all the time.

2 A friend of mine drinks eight cups of coffee a day – and __________ are usually big cups!

3 My boyfriend's addicted to working out at the gym. He goes __________ every day before work and five evenings a week.

4 Parents shouldn't smoke in front of their children. They have to teach __________ that smoking is very dangerous.

5 I'm trying to reduce the number of cigarettes I smoke. I never have __________ before lunch now.

# Review Unit 6

## EXERCISE 1

Read the extracts.

1 I'm writing to complain about a pair of shoes that I bought in one of your shops last month. I have only worn them on three occasions but …

2 … and by the way, I bought this amazing jacket the other day. It was only £3 in a second-hand clothes shop – I can't wait to show you!

3 If you are looking for souvenirs, Dorothy's Shop is the best option. It is in a quiet street behind the cathedral and …

4 • 20 hours playback • FM radio with 15 pre-sets • 40-second electronic skip protection • built-in recharge capacity • search/skip/program • batteries supplied • **£65.99**

## EXERCISE 2

**Match the extracts to these types of written language.**

| | |
|---|---|
| a catalogue: | extract number _____ |
| a guidebook: | extract number _____ |
| a formal letter: | extract number _____ |
| an email to a friend: | extract number _____ |

## EXERCISE 3

**Complete the sentences with *a, an, the* or *nothing*.**

1 Djemaa el Fna is _______ name of _______ main square.

2 _______ souk in _______ Marrakech has some fantastic products on offer.

3 A lot of _______ tourists visit _______ souk _______ every day.

4 You can buy _______ colourful rug, _______ leather jacket, or _______ delicous snack!

## EXERCISE 4

**Use an English-English dictionary and underline the correct word in bold in each of these short extracts.**

1 I saw a really lovely jacket when I was out shopping last week. I was going to buy it but then I looked at the price **tag / label / ticket**. It was £300!

2 I bought a shirt last week, but when I got it home, I noticed there was a mark on the back. I took it back to the shop and got a **return / repayment / refund.**

3 In the supermarket near my flat they're offering three bottles of champagne for the price of two. That's a really good **present / prize / bargain.**

4 If you buy something, you should always keep the **recipe / receipt / prescription**. You never know, you might want to take it back and change it.

5 If you go shopping at a market, you can often see the shoppers **hobbling / hurdling / haggling** with the stall-holders about the price of something.

# 7 Love and romance

**PRE-READING 1** **Look at the possible ways that people meet and fall in love. Give each one a mark from 1 to 10. 10 is *very romantic*, and 1 is *not romantic at all*.**

| | | | |
|---|---|---|---|
| at school | ____ | through a dating agency | ____ |
| at work | ____ | through a newspaper advert | ____ |
| on a bus or train | ____ | in a chatroom | ____ |
| at a party or nightclub | ____ | through friends / family | ____ |
| on holiday | ____ | arranged by parents | ____ |

**Look at the title of the text and the picture. Answer the questions.**

**1** What is speed dating? **2** What type of people do it?

**PRE-READING 2** **Complete the sentences with the key words in bold from the text.**

**1** Dave is a very good ________. He planned and made all the arrangements for the party.

**2** If something is ________, it is not what usually happens and can make people feel uncomfortable.

**3** When I was younger, I used to wear a ________ with the name of my favourite rock band on it.

**4** No guy will ever be quite right for Judy. She's just too ________.

**5** ________ means *possible in the future*.

**6** A ________ is a talk between two or more people.

**7** ________ are people who take part in something.

**8** Jenny and Dave are a very nice ________.

# Speed dating – three minutes to meet your match

**A** These days it seems to be impossible for some people to find the partner of their dreams. Perhaps people are spending too much time at work, or perhaps they are just too **choosy**, but whatever the reason, more and more men and women are using dating services to help them find love. Speed dating is the latest craze, and we asked Luigi, an **organizer** of speed dating evenings in San Francisco, to tell us how it works.

**B** 'The idea of speed dating is that you meet as many **potential** partners as possible in an evening. People know that first impressions are very important and they don't want to waste time talking to the wrong person.'

**C** 'At a speed-dating evening, there is always an even number of **participants** and an equal number of men and women. This way you always have somebody to speak to. First of all, we give each man and each woman a **badge** with a number on it. When the "dating" begins, the two participants with button number one start at table number one. The two with button number two start at table number two, and so on. After a few minutes, a bell rings and the men stand up and move to the next table while the women stay where they are. The men have to move however much they are enjoying the **conversation** at the time.'

**D** 'Between each "date" you're allowed a minute to take notes about the person you've talked to. The evening continues until you've met everyone there. You have just enough time with each person to decide if you want to see them again. Everyone gives their notes to the organizers, and they make arrangements if a **couple** want to meet again. You only have contact with people you like and who like you. There is no need for difficult phone calls, or trying to avoid people you don't want to see.'

**E** Some people think that speed dating is **unnatural**. They say it makes first impressions too important and feel that people need time to get to know each other. Whatever they think, though, speed dating is very popular and it's coming to your town soon.

## COMPREHENSION 1 Read the text and match the questions (1–5) to the paragraphs (A–E).

1 What is the basic idea of speed dating? ____
2 What if I want to see people again? ____
3 Does everyone think speed dating is a good idea? ____
4 How do speed-dating evenings work? ____
5 Why do people need help to find love? ____

## COMPREHENSION 2 Read the text again and answer the questions.

1 In line 3, *the partner of their dreams* means ...
  **a** the perfect person to start a business with.
  **b** the perfect boyfriend or girlfriend.
  **c** somebody they knew in the past.

2 In lines 9 and 10, *the latest craze* is something that ...
  **a** is very popular at the moment.
  **b** people think is mad.
  **c** comes from the USA.

3 In lines 15 and 16, your *first impressions* are ...
  **a** the first words you say to somebody.
  **b** your first boyfriend or girlfriend.
  **c** what you think about somebody when you first meet them.

4 In line 16, *waste time* means ...
  **a** to not use time in a good way.
  **b** to use time to do good things.
  **c** to wait for something to happen.

5 In line 18, an *even number* is, for example ...
  **a** 1, 3, 5, or 7.
  **b** 5, 10, 15, or 20.
  **c** 2, 4, 6, or 8.

6 In line 19, *an equal number of,* means, for example ...
  **a** two men and three women.
  **b** three women and two men.
  **c** three men and three women.

7 In line 24, *a bell rings* means there is ...
  **a** a bright light.
  **b** a sudden noise.
  **c** music.

8 In line 28, when participants *take notes* they …

a write things on paper.
b ask more questions.
c exchange phone numbers.

9 In line 33, *have contact with* means …

a see or speak to again.
b touch.
c remember.

10 In line 35, if you try to *avoid* somebody you try …

a to see them.
b not to see them.
c to find their phone number.

## COMPREHENSION 3

**Some of the key words in the text can be used in a number of phrases. Underline the phrase that is not correct.**

1 a perfect *partner* / a business *partner* / a dance *partner* / a class *partner*

2 have got a *date* / make a *date* with someone / a holiday *date* / a blind *date*

3 be in *love* / fall in *love* / true *love* / broken *love*

4 a nice *couple* / a young *couple* / a *couple* of minutes / a new *couple* of shoes

5 *waste* your work / *waste* your time / *waste* your money / *waste* an opportunity

6 say a *conversation* / make *conversation* / take part in a *conversation* / a long *conversation*

**Now complete the sentences with the key words.**

1 The ________________ was about football all evening. I was really bored.

2 Sally's ________________ is called Steve. I don't think they're married.

3 Don't ________________ £20 on that old thing. It's broken.

4 Mary's very excited. She's got a ________________ with Tony tonight.

5 Jim never stops talking about Claire. She's the ________________ of his life.

6 Can I just say a ________________ of things before you go?

**Grammar**
Present simple

When we describe a process that happens often, we use the present simple.
*'...When the "dating"* ***begins****, the two participants with badge number one* ***start*** *at table number one. The two with badge number two* ***start*** *at table number two and so on. After a few minutes, a bell* ***rings*** *and the men* ***stand up*** *and* ***move*** *to the next table while the women* ***stay*** *where they are.'*

## GRAMMAR Complete the text about a traditional Christian wedding with the verbs in the box in the present simple. Remember to add *-s*, if necessary.

| walk | put | throw | wait | look after | arrive | leave | give |
|---|---|---|---|---|---|---|---|

The groom (**1**)___________ at the church before the bride. He (**2**)___________ at the altar at the front of the church with the best man. The best man is usually his brother or a friend, and he (**3**)___________ the rings. The bride (**4**)___________ down the centre aisle with her father. The father (**5**)___________ his daughter to her new husband.

The couple make their promises and (**6**)___________ on the rings. The priest pronounces them man and wife. When the newlyweds (**7**)___________ the church, all the guests(**8**)___________ confetti (small pieces of coloured paper) and cheer.

## SPEAKING Talk to a partner or in a group of three and answer the questions.

1. Do you think speed dating is a good idea?
2. Would you ever try speed dating or going to a dating service?
3. Do you think first impressions are very important?

# Effective *Skills*

**ACTIVATING THE TOPIC**

**You will read two extracts from a very famous story called *Jane Eyre*, from the Macmillan Readers series. The story begins in 1825. Complete the sentences about the first half of the story with the verbs in the box.**

| saves | teaches | loves | becomes | meets | tries | falls |
|---|---|---|---|---|---|---|

1 Jane Eyre, a poor girl, leaves school and ___________ to find a job as a governess.

2 She works as a governess in a big house called Thornfield Hall. She ___________ English, Maths, Geography, and Music to a young French girl called Adèle.

3 She ___________ Mr Rochester, the master of the house and Adèle's guardian. She is walking in the country. He ___________ from his horse and she helps him.

4 She enjoys life at Thornfield Hall and ___________ friends with Mr Rochester.

5 There is a fire at the house. Jane ___________ Mr Rochester's life. She realises that she ___________ him.

**SKIMMING AND SCANNING**

**It is the day after Jane saves Mr Rochester's life. Read the extract quickly and choose the best summary.**

1 Jane is angry with Mr Rochester for going away.

2 Jane is sad when she learns that Mr Rochester is married.

3 Jane is jealous when she learns that Mr Rochester has a special friend.

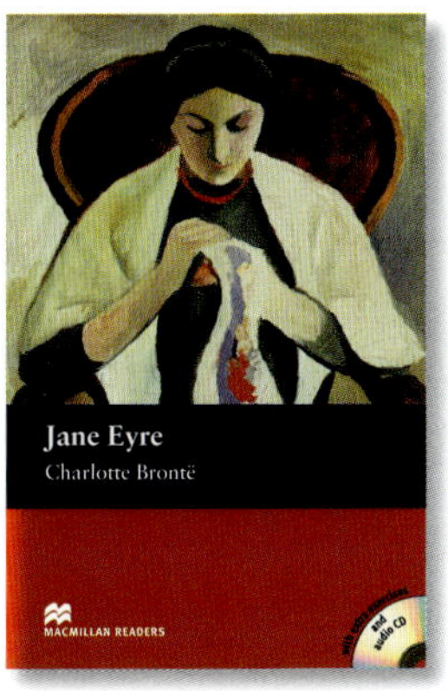


These extracts from *Jane Eyre* are taken from the Macmillan Readers series.

## *The day after the fire*

I did not see Mr Rochester the next day. He did not send for me.

In the evening, I went down to Mrs Fairfax's sitting-room. The housekeeper was looking out of the window.

'The weather has been good today,' Mrs Fairfax said. 'Mr Rochester had a good day for his journey.'

'His journey? Where has he gone?' I asked. I was surprised.

'He has gone to Ingram Park,' Mrs Fairfax replied. 'Mr Rochester will stay there for a week or more. He has many friends. All his friends will be at Ingram Park this week.'

'Will there be any ladies at Ingram Park?' I asked.

'Yes,' Mrs Fairfax said. 'There will be many ladies there. Miss Blanche Ingram will be there. Mr Rochester has known her for many years.'

'Is Miss Ingram beautiful?' I asked.

'She is very beautiful,' Mrs Fairfax said.

'Will Mr Rochester marry her?' I asked.

Mrs Fairfax smiled. 'I don't know, Miss Eyre,' she replied. 'I don't know.'

I was very unhappy. I went up to my bedroom. I looked in my mirror.

'Jane Eyre,' I said to myself. 'You are not pretty. And you are poor. Mr Rochester will never marry you. He will marry Miss Ingram. She is a rich lady. You are a poor governess. Forget Mr Rochester, Jane Eyre! Forget him!'

**READING FOR DETAIL**

**Read again more slowly and tick the sentences True (T), False (F), or the text Doesn't Say (DS).**

**1** Mrs Fairfax works at Thornfield Hall with Jane. T ☐ F ☐ DS ☐

**2** Jane knew that Mr Rochester was going away. T ☐ F ☐ DS ☐

**3** Jane knows Miss Ingram. T ☐ F ☐ DS ☐

**4** Mr Rochester is in love with Miss Ingram. T ☐ F ☐ DS ☐

**5** Mr Rochester is going to marry Miss Ingram. T ☐ F ☐ DS ☐

**6** Jane feels foolish to love Mr Rochester. T ☐ F ☐ DS ☐

**IDENTIFYING KEY PHRASES**

**Read this extract from later in the story. Put the key sentences into the spaces in the text.**

| | |
|---|---|
| He smiled at me | I walked into the garden |
| He was silent | I could not speak |
| Mr Rochester kissed me | I started to cry |

## *In the garden*

In June, the weather was hot. One evening, __________________. Mr Rochester was there too.

'Do you like this house, Jane?' he asked.

'Yes, sir,' I replied.

'Soon Adèle will go to live at a school, Jane,' he said. 'Then, I will not want a governess here. Will you be sad then, Jane? Will you leave Thornfield Hall?'

'Leave?' I said quickly. 'Must I leave Thornfield?'

'My dear – ' Mr Rochester stopped. __________________ for a moment. Then he said, 'I am going to be married soon.'

'Oh, sir,' I said. 'Then I must go far away. Far away from Thornfield. Far away from you, sir.' __________________.

'I will always remember you, Jane,' Mr Rochester said. 'Will you forget me?'

'No, sir,' I replied. 'I will never forget you. I don't want to leave Thornfield, sir. I don't want to leave you.'

'Don't leave, Jane,' Mr Rochester said. 'Stay here.' ____________________.

'I must not stay here, sir,' I said. 'You are going to marry Miss Ingram. I am poor. I do not have a pretty face. But I have a heart. It is a loving heart, sir!'

'Jane – I am not going to marry Miss Ingram.' Mr Rochester said. 'She is rich. She is beautiful. But I want to marry you! Will you marry me, Jane?'

For a moment, ____________________.

At last, I asked, 'Do you love me, sir?'

'I do,' he replied.

'Then, sir, I will marry you,' I said.

____________________.

## UNDERSTANDING DIALOGUE

**Complete the sentences from a love story with the correct verb.**

| told | thought | screamed | replied | asked |
|---|---|---|---|---|

1. 'Do you still love me?' Lucy ______________.
   'Of course, I do,' Martin ______________.
2. 'I'm afraid I'm in love with somebody else,' Daphne ______________ Eric.
3. 'Tomorrow I will tell her how I feel,' David ______________ to himself.
4. 'I hate you, I hate you!' Tamara ______________ at Edwin.

## SUMMARIZING A STORY

**Jane writes a letter to her uncle John to tell him her news. Complete the letter with some of the words in the box.**

| for | any | as | so | some | too | to | in | with | much |
|---|---|---|---|---|---|---|---|---|---|

*Dear Uncle,*

*I have __________ wonderful news. I'm going to be married. I am working __________ a governess at a big country house called Thornfield Hall. I am in love __________ the master of the house, Mr Rochester.*

*Yesterday he told me that he loved me __________ . We will be married ________ a month. I have never been __________ happy in my life.*

*I hope you are well and that you can come to the wedding.*

*Your loving niece,*

*Jane*

# 8 Cosmopolitan Europe

**PRE-READING 1** **Complete these sentences so they are true for you.**

1 A lot of people leave my country to live in ____________ and ____________.

2 ____________ is a town or city in my country where a lot of people from other countries live.

**You will read a text about Polish people leaving Poland to live in Britain. Underline one option in each pair that you think will appear in the text.**

1 an island near Scotland / a small town in Wales

2 Polish food and drink / Polish music

3 the Industrial Revolution / the Second World War

4 Polish soldiers / Polish pilots

5 the EU / the White House

**PRE-READING 2** **Look at the key words and phrases in bold in the text and underline the correct definition.**

1 **Immigrants** are *people who come to live in a country / unusual people.*

2 If something is **traditional**, *people don't know much about it / people have known about it for a long time.*

3 **Communities** are *people living together in a particular place / buildings.*

4 A **government** is the *group of people who control a country / an organization that helps people find a job.*

5 **Qualifications** show *where you come from / that you can do a job.*

6 **Migration** means *people moving from one country to another / countries joining the EU.*

7 **Unemployment** *is people not having a job / how much things cost.*

8 **Settlers** are people who *come to live in a new place / study together.*

# A little piece of Poland

**A** Llanelli is a small town in Wales much like any other small Welsh town. There is one thing that makes it unusual, though. 2,000 Polish **immigrants** have settled there in the last few years, and the population of 40,000 is now 5% Polish. Llanelli now has a delicatessen that sells only Polish food, and the local pub serves Polish lager along with more **traditional** Welsh beers.

**B** Poles have been coming to Britain for a long time and there are Polish **communities** all over the country. In 1939, at the beginning of the Second World War, thousands of Poles escaped the Nazis and came to Britain. When the war began, Britain had a shortage of pilots and many Polish pilots joined the British air force.

**C** When the war finished, a communist **government** was elected in Poland and large numbers of Poles decided not to return home. Many of them were doctors, lawyers and engineers, but they found it diffiult to find work because the Brtish didn't recognise their **qualifications**. As an alternative, they found work in the building trade or became coal miners. Some started businesses of their own, and there are still many Polish clockmakers and shoe repairers around the country.

**D** Now, at the beginning of the 21st century, there is another wave of **migration**. Poland became a member of the EU in 2004, and that gave Poles the freedom to work in Britain. **Unemployment** in Poland was high at that time, and many Poles took the opportunity to move to a place where there were more jobs and they could earn more money.

**E** In Llanelli, the relationship between the locals and the Polish **settlers** is good. Student Ana Kurek says, 'There will always be some problems when a large group of new people arrive in a small town, but the local people here are generally very friendly and I feel at home. Perhaps, when the situation in Poland is better, I'll want to go home, but for now I am very happy.'

## COMPREHENSION 1 Match the questions (1–5) to the paragraphs (A–E).

1 Why did Poles come to Britain in the last century? ____

2 Why are Poles coming to Britain now? ____

3 How do local people feel about immigrants coming to their towns? ____

4 How is one small town changing? ____

5 Why did Poles stay in Britain after the war? ____

## COMPREHENSION 2 Write True (T) or False (F) next to these facts from the text.

1 There are now 40,000 Poles in Llanelli. ____
2 Many Poles came to Britain in 1939. ____
3 After the war, most Poles had the jobs they wanted. ____
4 In 2004 it became easier for Poles to stay in Britain. ____
5 Ana Kurek wants to go back to Poland soon. ____

## COMPREHENSION 3 Read the text again and answer the questions.

**1** In line 3, *there* is …

- **a** in Llanelli
- **b** in Wales
- **c** in Poland

**2** In line 6, *along with* means …

- **a** in place of
- **b** for less money
- **c** as well as

**3** In line 11, a *shortage* means that there were …

- **a** no pilots
- **b** too many pilots
- **c** not enough pilots

**4** In line 11, if you *join the air force*, you …

- **a** drive tanks
- **b** fly planes
- **c** sail in ships

**5** In line 15, *didn't recognise* means …

- **a** couldn't understand
- **b** didn't accept as true
- **c** didn't see

**6** In line 16, *as an alternative* is like …

- **a** instead
- **b** because
- **c** too

7 In line 20, *another wave* says something about …

- **a** the sea
- **b** large numbers of people
- **c** saying goodbye

8 In line 26 *the locals* are …

- **a** the people of Llanelli
- **b** the police
- **c** Welsh students

9 In line 29, *generally* tells us that …

- **a** nobody is friendly
- **b** most people are friendly
- **c** everyone is friendly

## COMPREHENSION 4 These key words from the text are used in a new context. Underline the correct word in each sentence.

1. In winter there is a huge *shortage / migration* of birds from cold places to hot places.
2. I didn't like my job when I first started, but now I have *settled / escaped* into it very well.
3. Some politicians are not happy about the number of *immigrants / communities* who arrive in their country.
4. People are leaving the city because there is a *shortage / wave* of good schools.
5. The first *settlers / qualifications* in Australia found life very hard.
6. Alfred Hitchcock left his *government / home*, the UK, to make films in the USA.
7. Flamenco is the *home / traditional* music of Spain.
8. Nowadays, women have more *freedom / trade* than they did a hundred years ago.
9. Many young people face *unemployment / migration*.
10. When I travel to new places, I always eat what the *settlers / locals* are eating.

**Grammar**

Past simple – irregular verbs

Some verbs are irregular. The ending in the past simple of these verbs is not *-ed*.
Some of the most common verbs are irregular.
The only way to learn them is to read and remember them.

## GRAMMAR 1 Underline the irregular past simple form of these base verbs in the text and write them in the spaces.

| | | |
|---|---|---|
| **1** be (is) ________ | **5** can ________ | **9** come ________ |
| **2** be (are) ________ | **6** find ________ | **10** become ________ |
| **3** have ________ | **7** begin ________ | |
| **4** take ________ | **8** give ________ | |

### What are the past simple forms of these common irregular verbs?

| | | |
|---|---|---|
| **1** do ________ | **5** buy ________ | **9** put ________ |
| **2** go ________ | **6** speak ________ | **10** meet ________ |
| **3** get ________ | **7** take ________ | **11** leave ________ |
| **4** make ________ | **8** know ________ | **12** say ________ |

## GRAMMAR 2 Complete the story with verbs in the past simple.

My grandfather (**1**)__________ (be) from Ireland. He (**2**)__________ (leave) school when he was 15, and he (**3**)__________ (have) no qualifications. He (**4**)__________ (come) to London in the 1960s and (**5**)__________ (find) work as a builder. He soon (**6**)__________ (become) the boss and (**7**)__________ (make) a lot of money. He (**8**)__________ (buy) a big house in Chelsea. He (**9**)__________ (meet) my grandmother and they (**10**)__________ (get) married when they (**11**)__________ (be) both 20. They (**12**)__________ (have) six children. My mother is the youngest.

## SPEAKING Talk to a partner and answer the questions.

**1** Was there a time when a lot of people left your country to find work?
**2** Are there communities of people from other countries in your city?
**3** Do you know about any of their traditional events?

# Effective *Skills*

## ACTIVATING VOCABULARY

**Underline the correct words to make true sentences about your city. Use a dictionary to check the words and phrases in bold.**

1 Bars and clubs are *all around* / ***located*** *in one* ***area*** *of* the city.

2 I *never* / *don't usually* / *often* see **tourists** and **travellers** in bars and clubs.

3 **International DJs** *never* / *sometimes* / *often* play music in clubs.

4 There are *no* / *a few* / *a lot of* English and Irish pubs.

5 Famous **bands** *often* / *don't often* / *never* **perform live**.

6 There are *a lot of* / *a few* / *no* places where you can listen to **jazz**.

## SKIMMING AND SCANNING

**Read these sentences about nightlife in Prague. Read the text quickly and tick the two sentences that are true**

1 Prague has always been famous for its nightlife.

2 Young tourists like Prague because there are a lot of bars and clubs.

3 Most bars and clubs in Prague close before midnight.

4 All the clubs and bars are busy and play loud music.

5 Some people think the city was better before there was so much nightlife.

### Prague's explosion in nightlife

Prague, capital of the Czech Republic, is one of Europe's most beautiful cities and people have visited it for many years. Traditionally, tourists come to see the architecture, to see sights like the Charles Bridge, the Astronomical Clock and Prague Castle, and to enjoy operas and concerts at magnificent venues like the National Theatre. These days, however, just as many people come for the city's growing nightlife.

In Prague, a large number of bars and nightclubs are located in a small area close to the city centre, and they stay open until the early hours of the morning. Entrance to clubs is cheap; they charge around 50–100 Koruna (2–4) Euros), and once inside, alcohol is not expensive. All this attracts young tourists from Europe and other parts of the world.

*Radost FX* has been one of Prague's most popular clubs for a decade, and has done a lot to influence the city's music scene. DJs play house, techno, drum and bass and breakbeat. It has a café, a small art gallery and is very unusual inside. *Roxy* is very close to *Náměsti Republiky*, Prague's central square. International DJs play house, drum and bass, and famous bands like *Faithless* have performed here live.

If you prefer something more relaxing, there are excellent jazz clubs all over the city. *Reduta Jazz Club* has live performances by local and international musicians. At *Jazzboat* you can listen to Latin and blues as well as traditional jazz.

British travellers can feel at home in one of the many English or Irish pubs that have opened around the city. *The George and Dragon* serves English lager and fish and chips, and *The James Joyce* was the first Irish pub to open in Prague in 1993.

Not everyone is happy, though. There are concerns that tourism and the nightlife explosion is destroying the city's special atmosphere.

## RECOGNIZING NAMES IN A TEXT

**Read again more slowly and write the names into the correct spaces.**

1 three tourist attractions in Prague __________ __________ __________

2 a famous opera house __________

3 the currency (money used) of the Czech Republic __________

4 two popular nightclubs __________ __________

5 the main square in Prague __________

6 a famous band __________

7 two jazz clubs __________ __________

8 seven types of music __________ __________ __________
__________ __________ __________
__________

9 two British-style pubs __________ __________

## IDENTIFYING KEY WORDS

**Underline the correct word or phrase in each sentence and then write the key word in the space.**

1 The concert venues are *beautiful / not very nice*.
The key word in line 5 is ____________.

2 The clubs *give money to / take money from* the people who enter.
The key word in line 9 is __________.

3 *Radost FX* has been popular for *ten / twenty* years.
The key word in line 12 is __________.

4 *Radost FX* has *changed / destroyed* Prague's music scene.
The key word in line 13 is __________.

5 The jazz clubs make you *nervous / feel calm*.

The key word in line 17 is ________.

6 People are worried because there *isn't enough / is suddenly a lot of* nightlife.

The key word in line 26 is ________.

## UNDERSTANDING COMPOUND NOUNS

**You can understand compound nouns if you know the meaning of the two words that make them. Look again at these compounds from the text.**

nightlife nightclub city centre

**Match words in the two columns to make compounds. Is the meaning of each one clear?**

| | | | |
|---|---|---|---|
| 1 tooth | a dryer | 7 head | g shop |
| 2 bread | b book | 8 shoe | h man |
| 3 note | c room | 9 milk | i ache |
| 4 hair | d horse | 10 water | j shine |
| 5 class | e brush | 11 pocket | k fall |
| 6 race | f knife | 12 sun | l money |

## TAKING NOTES

**Complete the notes about the text. Put one word into each space. The words are not always in the text.**

1 Prague has always been a city that people like to ________.

2 Now more young people are coming because there are a lot of ________ and ________ in one part of the city.

3 The bars and clubs play a lot of different ________.

4 Clubs stay open all ________ and it is ________ to get in.

5 There are lots of jazz clubs where people can ________.

6 There are English and Irish ________ that serve traditional beer and ________.

7 Some people are worried that Prague is ________ too quickly.

# Review Unit 7

## EXERCISE 1

**Look at the T/F sentences first. Then read the text without a dictionary and complete the exercise as quickly as you can. Write your starting and finishing time.**

Time started: _______

### Arranged marriages

Arranged marriages are still the custom in India. Parents still help their sons and daughters find the right husband or wife, but the system is changing, especially in the bigger cities. In the past, parents decided whom their children would marry and the young couples didn't have much choice. These days, young men and women work together with their parents to find a partner. This is now often called an 'assisted marriage' rather than an 'arranged marriage'.

## EXERCISE 2

**Tick (✔) these sentences True (T), False (F), or the text Doesn't Say (DS).**

1 Arranged marriage in India is different now from how it was in the past.

T ☐ F ☐ DS ☐

2 In the past, young people could decide whom they wanted to marry.

T ☐ F ☐ DS ☐

3 In the past, couples married when they were very young.

T ☐ F ☐ DS ☐

4 These days, young people don't tell their parents whom they want to marry.

T ☐ F ☐ DS ☐

5 Arranged marriages are usually happy marriages.

T ☐ F ☐ DS ☐

Time finished: ________

## EXERCISE 3

**If you know the words in a new phrase, you can understand the phrase from the context. Read these short extracts without a dictionary and then underline the correct meaning.**

1 Jenny's new boyfriend isn't very good-looking, and he's so boring. I don't know **what she sees in him**.

The new phrase means *why she likes him / why she looks at him.*

2 Every time I see Mark and Maria, they have a big argument. He seems to spend more and more time away from the house. I think their marriage is **on the rocks.**

The new phrase means *going very well / going very badly.*

3 Ruth was very jealous when her husband started to come home late from work. She thought he was **having an affair**.

The new phrase means *working too hard at his office / having a relationship with another woman.*

4 As soon as I met my boyfriend, I knew he was the one for me. We **got on like a house on fire** from the first moment.

The new phrase means *had a very good relationship / had a very bad relationship.*

# Review Unit 8

### EXERCISE 1

**Read the text and see if you know the city. The answer is at the bottom of the page.**

## A weekend away

__________________ is one of the most popular cities in Europe for a weekend break. Young people come mainly for the nightlife. Clubs like *Powerzone* and *Melkweg* are among the best in Europe. Other people want to visit the art galleries. The *Rijksmuseum* has paintings by some of the most famous artists in history, and the Van Gogh Museum has the biggest collection of Van Gogh paintings in the world. If you are a football fan, you can go to see *Ajax* play a home game, and if you want to go ice-skating, the *Jaap Eden* is one of Europe's best rinks.

### EXERCISE 2

**Read again carefully and write the names into the spaces.**

1 two nightclubs

__________________ __________________

2 two famous art galleries

__________________ __________________

3 a famous artist

__________________

4 a football team

__________________

5 an ice rink

__________________

### EXERCISE 3

**Read the short texts and use the context to choose A, B, or C to answer the questions.**

1 If you're driving in the dark, you need to put your **headlights** on.

Headlights are …

**A** in the road.
**B** on your car.
**C** part of your body.

2 The position of women in the family has changed a lot. It is not always the man who is the main **breadwinner** these days.

The breadwinner …

**A** makes bread.
**B** cooks.
**C** earns the money.

3 Debbie is such a **bookworm**. Every time I see her, she tells me about a new novel she's reading.

A bookworm is …

**A** somebody who loves books.
**B** a small animal.
**C** somebody who works in library.

4 My aunt went into hospital for a **facelift** last month. She thinks it makes her look younger, but I think she looks really strange.

A facelift is …

**A** something you wear.
**B** a cream you put on your skin.
**C** a type of operation.

5 These days, most famous people have **bodyguards** with them whenever they go out in public.

A bodyguard …

**A** helps a famous person to look good.
**B** protects a famous person.
**C** drives a famous person's car.

The city is Amsterdam.

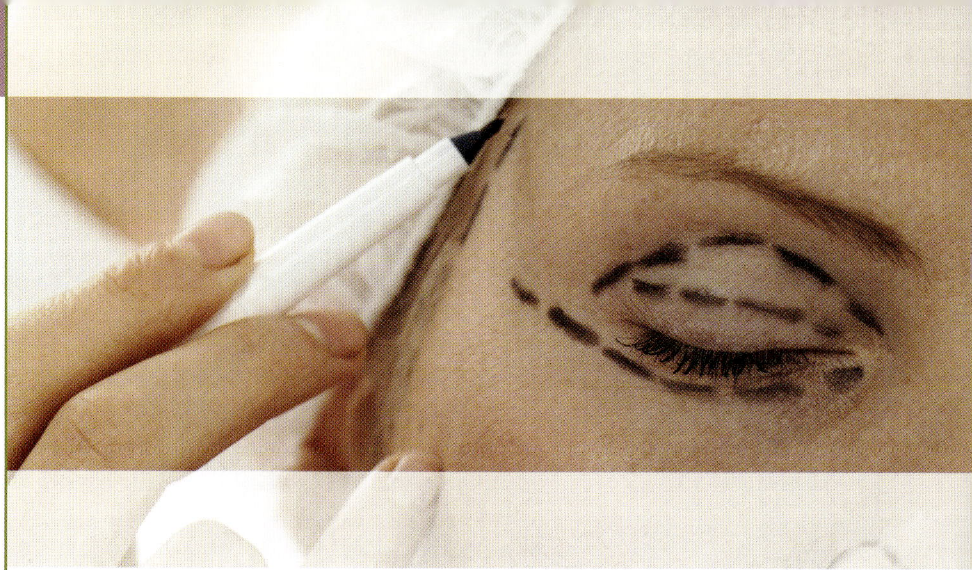

# 9 New faces

**PRE-READING 1** **A *transplant* is when doctors take a part of one person's body and put it in the body of another person. Decide if these transplants are possible. Tick (✔) yes or no.**

| | | yes | no | | | yes | no |
|---|---|---|---|---|---|---|---|
| 1 | heart transplant | ☐ | ☐ | 4 | liver transplant | ☐ | ☐ |
| 2 | brain transplant | ☐ | ☐ | 5 | head transplant | ☐ | ☐ |
| 3 | hand transplant | ☐ | ☐ | 6 | face transplant | ☐ | ☐ |

**PRE-READING 2** **Complete the sentences with the key words in bold from the text. Use each word only once.**

1 There are a lot of ______________ on this road. It's very dangerous.
2 A ______________ is a person who gives something to help another person.
3 I broke my leg last year. I had two ______________ in hospital but my leg is still not completely better.
4 My father needed ______________ on his heart. He was in hospital for three weeks.
5 A______________ is a doctor who does an operation in a hospital.
6 If a person is ______________ he or she looks different after an accident.
7 If you ______________ something, you say that you don't want it.
8 A number of ______________ were waiting to see the doctor.

# The UK's first face transplants

**A** A team of European **surgeons** is planning to do the first full face transplants very soon. This **surgery** hasn't been done anywhere in the world before. Doctors have worked on it for 14 years and believe that it is now possible. They say that it will improve the lives of many people who have been in **accidents**.

**B** The surgeons need volunteers to have the surgery. They have seen a number of possible **patients** but have not yet decided who will get the transplants. They are considering a young man of 22 whose face was burnt in a house fire, and a woman from Venezuela who was **disfigured** in a car crash.

**C** The first transplant of part of a human face took place last year in France on a woman who had been attacked by her dog. She received new lips, a new nose and a new chin. The **donor** had died in hospital earlier in the year. In China, doctors also claim to have performed a face transplant. They say they replaced part of the face of a man who was attacked by a bear.

**D** After the attack in France, it was difficult for the woman to eat and speak, but she now has feeling back in her face. She has to take drugs every day so that her body does not **reject** the new face, but doctors are satisfied with the operation.

**E** One of the European surgeons said, 'We have done everything possible to prepare for this surgery, and now **operations** must go ahead. Of course, it is difficult psychologically for the patient to have somebody else's face, but some people never leave their house because they don't want to show their face. We can give them a new life.'

## COMPREHENSION 1 Choose the main idea of each paragraph. Tick (✔) 1 or 2.

**Para A**

1 A lot of people have accidents. ☐

2 Doctors are ready to perform face transplants. ☐

**Para B**

1 Doctors need to find people to have the first transplant. ☐

2 There are a lot of car crashes in Venezuela. ☐

**Para C**

1 Dogs and bears are dangerous animals. ☐

2 In other countries, there have been face transplants. ☐

**Para D**

**1** The operation in France went well. ☐

**2** The woman in France has a problem with drugs. ☐

**Para E**

**1** It is important to give some people a new face. ☐

**2** People who want a new face are mad. ☐

## COMPREHENSION 2 Read the text again and answer the questions.

**1** In lines 1 and 2, *full face transplants* means …

**a** some of the face will be different.
**b** most of the face will be different.
**c** all of the face will be different.

**2** In line 6, the doctors *need volunteers* means that they need …

**a** help.
**b** people.
**c** more money.

**3** In line 8, *they are considering a young man of 22* means that …

**a** he will have the operation.
**b** he might have the operation.
**c** he will not have the operation.

**4** In line 10, *a car crash* is …

**a** an accident.
**b** a type of car.
**c** a journey.

**5** In line 13, *lips* and *chin* are …

**a** types of dog.
**b** parts of a face.
**c** things to wear.

**6** In line 14, if you *claim* something, you say that …

**a** something is true.
**b** something was difficult.
**c** you didn't do something.

**7** In line 20, *satisfied with* means …

**a** surprised about.
**b** unhappy about.
**c** happy about.

**8** In line 22, if you *prepare for* something, you …

**a** get ready.
**b** do it.
**c** stop it.

**9** In lines 22 and 23, *go ahead* means …

**a** begin.
**b** stop.
**c** change.

**10** In line 23, *it is difficult psychologically* means …

**a** it hurts a lot.
**b** it is difficult to think about and understand.
**c** it costs a lot.

## COMPREHENSION 3 Complete the story with these words from the text.

| hospital | burnt | operation | accident | surgeon | improve | patients |
|---|---|---|---|---|---|---|

When I was 10 years old I had a bad (**1**)____________. I was in the kitchen and I pulled a very hot pan of water off the cooker. It (**2**)____________ one of my arms very badly. My mother and father took me to the (**3**)____________, where I stayed for three days. I wanted to go home, but the other (**4**)____________ were friendly and made me feel better.

When my condition started to (**5**)____________, the doctors said I could go home, but I wasn't happy. My arm looked horrible, and I didn't want people to see it. At the hospital, they said I could have a special (**6**)____________. The (**7**)____________ explained that they could take skin from the top of my leg and put it on my arm. They did the operation, and now my arm looks perfect.

**Grammar**
Clauses with *who*

We use the pronoun *who* to join clauses in a sentence when we are talking about people. *Who* replaces the subject pronoun.

*(There was a man. He was attacked by a bear.) … a man* ***who*** *was attacked by a bear.*
*NOT … a man who he was attacked by a bear.*

## GRAMMAR 1 Match the two parts of each definition (1–4 to a–d).

| | | | |
|---|---|---|---|
| **1** | A nurse is a person | **a** | who gives a body part to help somebody else. |
| **2** | A patient is a person | **b** | who does operations in hospital. |
| **3** | A surgeon is a doctor | **c** | who is ill in hospital. |
| **4** | A donor is somebody | **d** | who looks after patients in hospital. |

## GRAMMAR 2 Complete the sentences with *who* in **one** of the two spaces.

**1** The woman ______ had the transplant in France ______ is called Isabelle Dinoire.

**2** Jean-Michel Dubernard ______ is the surgeon ______ did the transplant in France.

**3** There are not many surgeons ______ in the world ______ can do this kind of operation.

**4** A boy ______ lost one of his ears in an accident ______ is going to have an operation to replace it.

## GRAMMAR 3 Use *who* to make one sentence from the two sentences.

**1** Peter is a boy. He plays football with me.

Peter is ________________________________________.

**2** Mrs Andrews is a woman. She works with my father.

Mrs Andrews is ________________________________________.

## SPEAKING Talk to a partner and answer the questions.

**1** Will a lot of people have face transplants in the future?

**2** Will people have face transplants just to be beautiful?

# Effective Skills

**ACTIVATING VOCABULARY**

**Check the correct definition for *cosmetic surgery* in your dictionary.**

**A** surgery that repairs part of a person's body after an accident

**B** surgery that people want to have to change how they look

**PREDICTING**

**You will read a text about teenagers having cosmetic surgery. <u>Underline</u> the answer that you think is correct in the sentences. Use a dictionary to check words that you don't know.**

1. People under 18 can't *have* / *are having* cosmetic surgery.
2. *Not many* / *about half* of teenagers in Britian have considered having cosmetic surgery.
3. Some Asian girls want their *eyes* / *lips* to look bigger.
4. Some Asian parents *want* / *don't want* their daughters to have operations.
5. Young people copy other *teenagers* / *famous people*.

**SKIMMING AND SCANNING**

**Read the text quickly and match the ideas (1-4) to the paragraphs (A-D).**

1. Many different operations are possible. ____
2. Some operations aren't very expensive. ____
3. Cosmetic surgery can make you feel good about yourself. ____
4. Not only older people want cosmetic surgery. ____

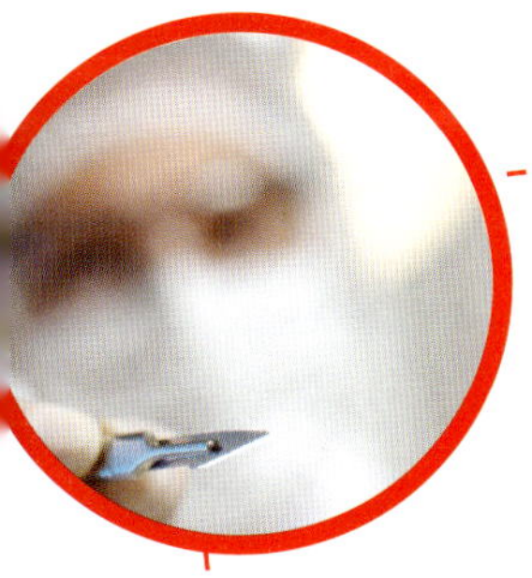

## Teens want cosmetic surgery

**A** For a long time, cosmetic surgery was done to middle-aged people who wanted to keep their young looks. These days, however, across the world, it is teenagers that are **obsessed** with having their faces and bodies **reshaped**. In fact, in the U.S. last year, nearly a quarter of a million patients under the age of 18 had a cosmetic operation.

**B** A recent survey in Britain showed that one in three teenagers would like to have cosmetic surgery, and that nearly half have at least thought about it. 15 and 16-year-olds have considered operations that reshape their nose, **enlarge** their lips, remove fat from various parts of their body or reduce their **tummies** and make them look thinner.

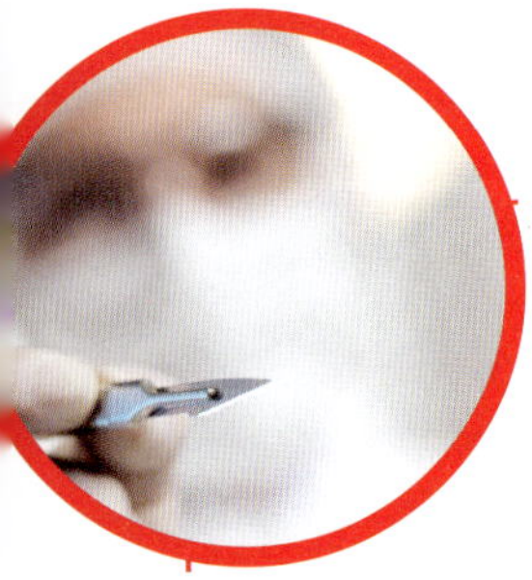

**C** In many parts of Asia, girls are obsessed with their eyes. Chinese and Korean girls dream of having bigger eyes, and it's now possible with a simple operation that costs only $700. A small cut is made above the eye to make an **artificial** double eyelid. Girls as young as 14 are having the operation, and it is now a common high school graduation gift from **proud** parents.

**D** Nowadays, some teenagers feel that improving their looks improves their **self-esteem**, and they think that having operations is perfectly normal. Many believe that these operations should be free, but most of them would be happy to pay for surgery. Young people copy adults, especially famous ones. Since more and more **celebrities** are having surgery, more and more teenagers are doing the same.

## READING FOR DETAIL

**Read again more slowly and mark the sentences True (T) or False (F).**

1 In the past, most cosmetic surgery was done to make people look younger. T ☐ F ☐

2 Most British teenagers plan to have cosmetic surgery. T ☐ F ☐

3 Eyelid operations are expensive and difficult to do. T ☐ F ☐

4 In Asia, parents often pay for their daughters to have eye operations when they graduate from high school. T ☐ F ☐

5 Some teenagers think that looking good means feeling good. T ☐ F ☐

6 The text implies that a lot of famous people have surgery. T ☐ F ☐

## VOCABULARY IN CONTEXT 1

**Write words in bold in the text into the spaces in these definitions.**

1 If something is ____________, it is made by people and is not natural.

2 If you feel ____________, you are pleased about something that you or somebody that you know did well.

3 If something is ____________, it is made to look different.

4 People know ____________ because they see them on TV and in newspapers.

5 If you are ____________ with something, you think about it all the time.

6 When women are expecting a baby, their ____________ get bigger.

7 If you ____________ something, you make it bigger.

8 If you have ______, you are confident and feel good about yourself.

## VOCABULARY IN CONTEXT 2

**You know *look* and *cut* as verbs, but in the text they are used as nouns. You can probably understand them in context – read lines 2 and 13 again.**

**Now use these common verbs as nouns in the sentences.**

| go | make | play | walk | smoke |
|---|---|---|---|---|

**1** It's a lovely day. Let's go for a _________ in the park.

**2** That's a very nice camera. What _________ is it?

**3** We went to the theatre to see a Shakespeare _________.

**4** There was a lot of black _________ coming from the fire.

**5** That computer game looks good. Can I have a _________?

## IDENTIFYING KEY FACTS

**Complete the notes with one or two words in each space. The words are not always in the text.**

1 *All over the world, _________ are having cosmetic surgery.*

2 *Around 250,000 teenagers had operations in _________ last year.*

3 *In Britain, 50% of teenagers have considered having an _________.*

4 *Many want surgery that makes their noses look different or their lips look _________. Others want _________ removed so that they look thinner.*

5 *In Asia, it is common for girls to have operations on _________. The operations are simple and _________ very much to have done.*

6 *Teenagers think that having cosmetic surgery is a _________ thing to do. They see _________ people doing it, and _________ them.*

# 10 International sport

**PRE-READING 1** **Answer the questions. Use a dictionary to check the words in bold.**

1 Can you name three European football **clubs**?

_______________ _______________ _______________

2 Can you name the **coach** of any big European team?

_______________ _______________ _______________

3 Can you name three **footballers** from outside Europe who are playing in Europe?

_______________ _______________ _______________

4 Can you name three Manchester United players?

_______________ _______________ _______________

**PRE-READING 2** **Check *adapt to* in your dictionary. Here are some things that Asian football players need to adapt to if they play in Europe. Match the verbs (1–5) to the phrases (a–e).**

| | | | |
|---|---|---|---|
| **1** | speaking | **a** | other players in the team / the coach |
| **2** | eating | **b** | their picture in the newspapers |
| **3** | playing | **c** | a new language |
| **4** | talking to | **d** | in front of bigger crowds |
| **5** | seeing | **e** | different food |

**PRE-READING 3** **Complete the sentences with these key football words in bold from the text. Use a dictionary.**

| armband | captain | tactics | substitutes | league |
|---|---|---|---|---|

1 The _____________ always leads his team onto the football pitch.

2 The captain wears an _____________ so that other people know he is the captain.

3 A team can bring on three _____________ during the match.

4 A team are the champions if they finish top of their ____________.

5 The coach explains the ____________ to his players before a match.

**Now match these definitions with the other three key words in bold in the text.**

6 extremely important ____________

7 express your thoughts and feelings to other people ____________

8 something that you want to achieve ____________

## European football – an international melting-pot

The best footballers have the **ambition** to play for the best teams, and the top sides in the Spanish, Italian, English and German **leagues** are now made up of players from every corner of the globe. Players, like Maradona and Ronaldinho, have been coming from South America to play in Europe for many years, but now there are players from Asia, Africa and the Middle East, too. Perhaps the most international league of all is the English Premiership. Chelsea currently have players from sixteen different countries, and last season Arsenal played a match without a single English player in the starting eleven.

So, how do players from outside Europe adapt to being in a new environment, surrounded by so many new faces? How do they make the most of their ability, when they have so many other things to worry about? Some players do not adapt; they play badly, and they lose their place in the team. It is **crucial** that the clubs help them to feel at home and enjoy their new lives.

When players arrive in Europe, they have to learn a new language and get used to very different food. However, the hardest thing for some of them to adapt to is the way players **communicate** with each other and with the coach. In Asia, for example, players don't complain if their team mates play badly, and they never tell the coach they are unhappy about **tactics**. In Europe, it is usual for players to say what they think.

The Korean international, Park Ji-Sung, learnt about the importance of communication in one of his early games for Manchester United. Late in the match, he came on as a **substitute** for Ryan Giggs, who was the **captain** that night. Giggs passed the captain's **armband** to Park, and wanted him to give it to another player, Rio Ferdinand. Park didn't understand, and he put the armband on. He played for the last seven minutes as the captain. The next day, all the newspapers wanted Park to tell them what it was like to be the captain of Manchester United.

**COMPREHENSION 1** **Read the text and underline the correct word or phrase in each sentence.**

1 Many English football clubs have a lot of *English / foreign* players.

2 Footballers from around the world have *some problems / no problems* when they come to play in Europe.

3 The players' new clubs *must / don't need* to help them to adapt.

4 Asian players find it *natural / difficult* to tell people what they really think.

5 *Ryan Giggs / Park Ji-sung* was the captain at the start of the match.

6 The coach planned for *Rio Ferdinand / Park Ji-sung* to be the captain for the last seven minutes.

7 Park Ji-sung put on the armband because he *thought he should be the captain of Manchester United / made a mistake*.

**COMPREHENSION 2** **Read the text again and answer the questions.**

1 In line 2, *top sides* means …

- **a** best players.
- **b** best teams.
- **c** nicest cities.

2 In line 3, *every corner of the globe* means …

- **a** all over the world.
- **b** near to where they were born.
- **c** the best football academies.

3 In line 8, *last season* means …

- **a** very recently.
- **b** about a year ago.
- **c** ten years ago.

4 In line 9, *the starting eleven* means …

- **a** all the players at a club.
- **b** the best players at a club.
- **c** the players in the team at the beginning of a match.

5 In line 15, *feel at home* means …

- **a** feel relaxed and comfortable in a new place.
- **b** want things from your own country.
- **c** play football well.

6 In line 17, *get used to* means …

a become familiar with.
b eat a lot of.
c learn how to cook.

7 In line 19, *players don't complain* means …

a they don't look for a new club.
b they don't walk off in the middle of a match.
c they don't say what they are unhappy about.

8 In lines 19 and 20 *their team mates* are …

a players on the same team.
b players on the other team.
c the referee and his assistants.

9 In line 23, *one of his early games* tells us …

a the game started before other games.
b it was at the start of the game.
c it was one of Park Ji-sung's first games for the club.

## COMPREHENSION 3

**Some of the key words in the text can be used in a number of phrases. Underline the phrase that is not correct.**

1 a tennis club / an after-school club / a political club /a nightclub

2 a baseball team / a team of lawyers / a team of elephants / a team of horses pulling a carriage

3 the baseball season / the rainy season / the tourist season / the school season

4 the captain of a basketball team / the captain of our department / the captain of a ship / a captain in the police

5 a game of tennis / a game of cards / a game show / a beauty game

**Use the words in the box to correct the phrases above. Write the phrases in the spaces below.**

| herd | contest | ~~party~~ | term | head |
|---|---|---|---|---|

***For example:***

*a political party*

1 ______________________

2 ______________________

3 ______________________

4 ______________________

**Grammar**

**Superlative adjectives**

We use superlatives to compare people or things with all the other people or things within a topic area.

***the hardest** thing to adapt to is …*
*one of Korea's **most popular** sportsmen*
*many of **the best** Asian football players*

Here are some rules for forming superlatives:
the + short adjective + *-est* (the tallest, the coldest)
the + short adjective + double letter + *-est* (the biggest, the hottest)
the + adjective ending in -y + *-iest* (the happiest, the busiest)
the + most + long adjective (the most difficult, the most interesting)

*Good* and *bad* have irregular superlatives *best* and *worst.*

## GRAMMAR Complete the information using the adjectives as superlatives.

| important | surprising | old | young | easy | good | big | quick |
|---|---|---|---|---|---|---|---|

1 ____________ player to score a goal in a World Cup final was Pelé of Brazil. He scored two goals against Sweden in 1958 when he was just 17.

2 ____________ football player to play in the World Cup was Roger Milla. He was 42 when he played for Cameroon in 1994.

3 Turkey's Hakan Sukur scored ____________ goal in World Cup history, against South Korea. He scored after only 11 seconds.

4 The Maracana stadium in Brazil is ____________ stadium in the world. A crowd of 199,854 people watched the 1950 World Cup final there.

5 ____________ date for English football fans is 30 July, 1966. England beat Germany 4-2 to win the World Cup for the only time.

6 In the 1982 World Cup, Hungary had ____________ match. They beat El Salvador 10-1.

7 Perhaps, ____________ result in World Cup history was when North Korea beat Italy 1-0 in 1966.

8 Many people think that Brazil's Pelé and Diego Maradona of Argentina are ____________ football players of all time.

## SPEAKING Talk to a partner. If you like football, answer the first three questions. If you don't like football, answer the other two questions.

1 Do you support a football team?

2 When did you start supporting them? Why?

3 Who is your favourite football player? Why?

4 Why don't you like football?

5 What sports do you like playing or watching?

# Effective • *Skills*

**PREDICTING**

**Look at the picture of the golfer Annika Sörenstam. Do you know anything about her? Underline the information that you think is correct. Use a dictionary to check the words in bold.**

1 Annika Sörenstam is from *Denmark / Sweden*.
2 She has earned *£10 million / £5 million*.
3 She started playing golf when she was *9 / 12 years old*.
4 The best thing about her game is *her long* ***drive*** */ the* ***accuracy*** *of her shots*.
5 Her **putting** *is / isn't* very good.
6 She plays *only in women's* ***tournaments*** */ in women's and men's tournaments*.

**SKIMMING AND SCANNING**

**Read the text quickly and put the key nouns into the correct spaces.**

| golf | golfers | clubs | score | business | tournaments |
|---|---|---|---|---|---|

## Annika Sörenstam – the top lady in golf

Not everyone has heard of Annika Sörenstam, but she is perhaps the best female golfer of all time. The Swede has won 69 official ladies' ________ , including ten **majors**, and in 2003, she made history as the first woman for nearly 60 years to play in a major men's event.

She has earnt over £10 million, £3.5 million more than her nearest **rival**. In ladies' ________ she is so famous that she is known simply as *Annika*, like Tiger Woods is known only as *Tiger.*

Annika is not especially tall, and she drives a golf ball only about 265 yards. She relies on the accuracy of her shots and her excellent putting. She is the only woman to shoot a ________ of 59 while playing in a tournament. When she entered the men's tournament, her friend Tiger Woods said, 'I think she wants to know if the **gap** between men's and women's golf is really so big.'

Annika was born in Bru near Stockholm in1970. As a girl, she was an excellent tennis player, and she was such a **promising** skier that she nearly became a professional. She first took up golf when she was 12. She shared her first set of ________ with her sister, Charlotta, who also became a **professional** golfer.

As she approaches 40, Sörenstam is spending more time on her ________ interests. Her first **design** for a golf course, *the Annika Course,*

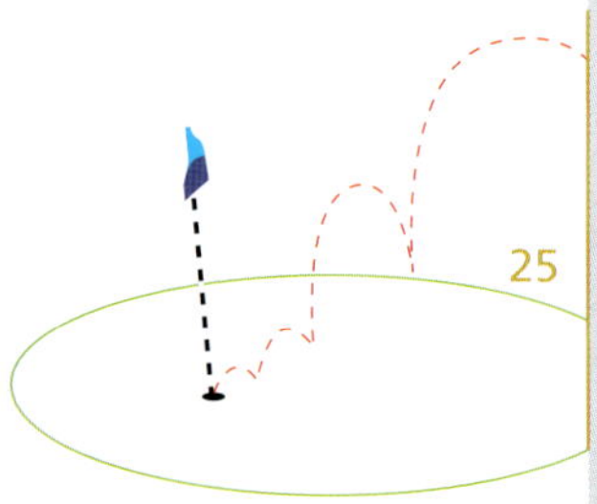

opened in Hong Kong in 2003, and her second opened in South Africa in 2008. In 2007, she started a golf academy, the *Annika Academy*, which she now runs with her sister.

Younger female ________ are getting better all the time. She may not win many more major tournaments, but Annika Sörenstam has a lot to look forward to.

## READING FOR DETAIL

**Tick the sentences True (T), False (F), or the text Doesn't Say (DS).**

1 Women often compete with men in major golf tournaments. T ☐ F ☐ DS ☐
2 Annika played very well in the men's tournament. T ☐ F ☐ DS ☐
3 Annika is the richest female golfer in the world. T ☐ F ☐ DS ☐
4 Annika can hit a golf ball further than most male golfers. T ☐ F ☐ DS ☐
5 Tiger Woods thinks Annika can win a men's tournament. T ☐ F ☐ DS ☐
6 Annika was very good at skiing when she was younger. T ☐ F ☐ DS ☐
7 Annika and her sister used the same golf clubs. T ☐ F ☐ DS ☐
8 Annika teaches young people how to play golf. T ☐ F ☐ DS ☐
9 A lot of young female golfers are now better than Annika. T ☐ F ☐ DS ☐

## VOCABULARY IN CONTEXT 1

**Complete the sentences with the words and phrases in bold in the text.**

1 Football clubs sometimes pay a lot of money for very ____________ seven and eight-year olds.
2 A big ____________ opened up between the runners.
3 I love the ____________ of the new stadium. It's so modern.
4 On the golf course, she is my biggest ____________. Off the course, we are great friends.
5 My sister stopped working as a nurse to become a ____________ tennis player. She makes much more money now.
6 __________ are the biggest tournaments, and every player wants to win them.

## MALE OR FEMALE WORDS

**Underline words in the text that are used only for males or only for females. Mark them (M) male or (F) female.**

***For example:***

Not everyone has heard of Annika Sörenstam but she (F)…

## VOCABULARY IN CONTEXT 2

**You know *drive* a car, but in line 9 *drive* means *hit a golfball a long way* (usually with a wooden golf club).**

**Now use these common verbs in new ways.**

| eat run read drink pull |
|---|

1 Big cars ____________ a lot of petrol.
2 Ronaldinho can always ____________ a big crowd when he plays.
3 My children are lovely but they ____________ up a lot of my time.
4 The best football players can ____________ the game and know what is going to happen.
5 In my country the trains always ____________ late on Sundays.

## CORRECTING ERRORS

**Delete eight unnecessary words in the notes.**

*Annika Sörenstam is a very successful female golfer. She has won many tournaments and then made a lot of money. She plays in touraments against the men.*

*She is not very much tall and doesn't hit a golf ball as far as most male golfers. Her shots are too accurate, though, and her putting is very good.*

*Annika was a very good tennis player and skier, but she started playing a golf when she was at 12 years old. Her sister also is a professional golfer, too.*

*Annika is a successful business woman. She has designed golf courses, and runs an academy for some young golfers.*

**Now write a few lines about a sportsman or woman that you really like.**

*I really like* ________________________________________

*because* ________________________________________

________________________________________

# Review Unit 9

## EXERCISE 1

**Read the text without a dictionary and complete the exercise as quickly as you can. Write your starting and finishing time.**

Time started: ________

### Living Doll

Cindy Jackson has had more cosmetic surgery than any other person ________________. Her face is very different from the face she had ________________ in 1988. She has had four facelifts and three operations to change the shape of her eyes. She has had surgery to make her nose smaller, and surgery to reduce the size of her chin. She has had implants ________________ and her teeth have been made whiter. She has also had many other operations ________________ of her body. Cindy has spent £50,000 ________________ and she hasn't finished yet.

## EXERCISE 2

**Now put these phrases with the prepositions into the spaces.**

| in her lips | on cosmetic surgery |
|---|---|
| on other parts | in the world |
| before her first operation | |

Time finished: ________

## EXERCISE 3

**Delete the one word which is not a part of your face.**

eyes

eyelids

facelift

nose

chin

teeth

lips

## EXERCISE 4

**In each pair of sentences decide if the word in bold is a noun (N) or verb (V).**

1 I think my girlfriend has a really lovely **face**. ____

I've got a terrible headache. I don't think I can **face** work today. ____

2 **Smile**! I'm going to take a picture. ____

Look at this picture. Why has Martin got such a big **smile** on his face? ____

3 Romantic films always make me **cry**. ____

We heard a **cry** and ran to see what was happening. ____

4 I thought the **end** of the film was a bit disappointing. ____

So, how did the story **end**? ____

5 I don't want you tell me any more **lies**. ____

I don't trust Jason. He **lies** to everyone. ____

6 When did you learn to **drive**? ____

Their house is at the end of a beautiful **drive** with trees on both sides. ____

# Review Unit 10

## EXERCISE 1

**Read the text without a dictionary.**

### The Golden Girl of Tennis

Maria Sharapova has not actually won very many major tennis tournaments but that doesn't stop her being the richest woman in sport. She is also the world's highest earning tennis player, making more than men's number one, Roger Federer. The Russian makes most of her $25 million a year from advertising and sponsorship deals. Sharapova is a beautiful woman, and this makes her perfect for advertising products like cars and watches. She has also just launched her own perfume. One day, Sharapova could make even more than Formula 1 superstar Michael Schumacher, who made £40 million in 2005.

## EXERCISE 2

**Choose A, B, or C to answer the questions.**

1 Maria Sharapova is extremely rich because …

**A** she is the best female tennis player in the world.

**B** a lot of companies want her to advertise their products.

**C** she wins a lot of big tournaments.

2 Roger Federer …

**A** is the best male tennis player in the world.

**B** is richer than Maria Sharapova.

**C** also makes most of his money from advertising.

3 Michael Schumacher is mentioned in this text because …

**A** he is a great Formula 1 driver.

**B** he also advertises a lot of products.

**C** he is richer than Maria Sharapova.

## EXERCISE 3

**Look at the words in the box and use them in the sentences. Be careful about plurals – some of them are irregular!**

| sportsman like sportswear sporting sports sportsman sportswoman |
|---|

1 The World Cup and the Olympic games are the biggest ____________ events of modern times.

2 I prefer team ____________ like football and basketball.

3 Joe is a very keen ____________. He plays tennis, baseball, and volleyball. He's even good at boxing.

4 In football these days, it is ____________ to kick the ball off the field if a player from the other team is down on the ground.

5 Martina Navratilova was a great tennis player – in fact, she was one of the greatest ____________ in history.

6 When I'm at work I wear a suit, so when I'm at home I like sitting around in ____________. It's much more comfortable.

# 11 Changing pop music

**PRE-READING 1** **Answer the questions about the music you listen to. Use a dictionary to check the words in bold.**

1 What is your favourite **type** of music? ____________________
2 Which **band** is your favourite? ____________________
3 Who is the **lead singer** of the band? ____________________
4 What is your favourite **album**? ____________________
5 What is your favourite **track** on it? ____________________
6 Do you ever go to **live concerts**? yes ☐ no ☐

**PRE-READING 2** **Look at the key words in bold in the text and underline the correct definition.**

1 A **graphic novel** is *a very serious book / a book of stories with pictures.*
2 A **virtual** rock band is *a real rock band / not a real rock band.*
3 **Animated characters** are *real people in the real world / people or animals that an artist draws.*
4 If something is **fictional**, *it really happens / it isn't true.*
5 A **recording studio** is a place where *musicians record songs / people can buy records.*
6 A **cartoon** is *a drawing / a model.*
7 **Guest singers** *sing at people's parties / sing on other musician's records.*
8 A **screen** is *like a thin wall / a musical instrument.*

# *Gorillaz* – a virtual pop group

In 1998, Damon Albarn, the lead singer of the popular British rock band *Blur*, decided that he wanted to do something different. At the same time Jamie Hewlett, the creator of the **graphic novel** *Tank Girl*, also felt that he wanted to do more than write comic stories. Together they decided to create a **virtual** pop band and call it *Gorillaz*. Now *Gorillaz* is known all over the world.

There are four **animated characters** in the virtual band: 2D, Murdoc, Noodle, and Russel. They play every type of music from rap and hip-hop to heavy metal. 2D is the singer and keyboard player; Murdoc is the bass player; Russel, from New York, is the drummer; and Noodle is the teenage Japanese guitarist. At first she could say only one word in English, which was 'noodle'.

*Gorillaz* made their first record in 2000, and it was a huge success. Hewlett created an animated video story for each of the four tracks on the record. People could also get a pamphlet that told the **fictional** story of the band. The band's website became very popular, too. People could visit the **recording studio** and the homes of all of the characters. It was even possible to get onto each of the character's computers to find out more about them. Everyone wanted to know who was behind the **cartoon** pop band.

In 2001, the band's first album, called simply *Gorillaz*, sold more than 3 million copies, and people soon learnt that Damon Albarn was the man behind the music. This made *Gorillaz* even more popular, and the second album, *Demon Days*, became the number one album within the first week of its release. Famous **guest singers** sang on some of the tracks.

Albarn and Hewlett wanted *Gorillaz* to play at some live concerts, but it was difficult to decide how to do it. In the end, the cartoon characters were projected onto a huge **screen** while real musicians played behind it.

Now Damon Albarn says that *Gorillaz* have gone as far as they can go, and there will not be a third album.

## COMPREHENSION 1 Read the text quickly and say which one sentences is true.

1 Damon Albarn is the lead singer of a real band called *Gorillaz*.

2 Jamie Hewlett stopped playing in a band so he could write graphic novels.

3 Two men created a virtual rock band that became very popular.

4 Nobody knows that Damon Albarn is behind *Gorillaz*.

5 *Gorillaz* doesn't play at live concerts.

6 *Gorillaz* has made three very popular albums.

## COMPREHENSION 2 Read the text again and answer the questions.

1 In line 2, *Blur* is the name of …

- a a rock band.
- b a person.
- c a comic.

2 In lines 3 and 4, if Jamie Hewlett was the *creator* of *Tank Girl* …

- a he invented it.
- b he was a character in it.
- c he was a person who reads graphic novels.

3 In line 13, *it was a huge success* means …

- a people didn't like it.
- b it was very popular.
- c it was longer than a usual record.

4 In line 15, a *pamphlet* is something you …

- a listen to.
- b read.
- c watch.

5 In line 20, *was behind* means …

- a was slower than others.
- b wasn't in front.
- c was the creator.

**6** In lines 24 and 25, *became the number one album* means …

- **a** it was the first album made.
- **b** it was the only album made.
- **c** it sold more than any other album at the time.

**7** In line 29 if the characters *were projected,* they were …

- **a** painted.
- **b** shown by a machine.
- **c** tied to part of the stage.

**8** In lines 31 and 32, … *have gone as far as they can go* means …

- **a** this is the time to stop.
- **b** are very good.
- **c** are boring.

## COMPREHENSION 3 Write words from the text in the second column.

| root word | person |
|---|---|
| 1 play | player |
| 2 sing | ______ |
| 3 guitar | ______ |
| 4 drum | ______ |
| 5 create | ______ |
| 6 music | ______ |

### How many of these questions can you answer? Underline one option.

**1** Luciano Pavarotti is *an opera singer / a rock singer.*

**2** Ringo Starr was the *guitarist / drummer* in the *Beatles.*

**3** *U2's* bass player is *Bono / Adam Clayton.*

**4** *Walt Disney / Alfred Hitchcock* was the creator of Mickey Mouse.

**5** Bob Marley was a *musician / tennis player.*

### Write the nouns of these words from the text. Use a dictionary to check.

**1** different ______

**2** popular ______

**3** animated ______

**4** fictional ______

**5** famous ______

**6** decide ______

**Grammar**
Verb patterns

Some verbs are often followed by another verb in the full infinitive form.
*… he **wanted to do** something different*
*… they **decided to create** a virtual pop band*

## GRAMMAR 1 Complete the sentences with the verbs in the infinitive.

play live get make read be

1 Damon Albarn doesn't **plan** _______ another *Gorillaz* album.
2 Most small rock bands **hope** _______ famous one day.
3 My brother **wants** _______ in a rock band when he leaves university.
4 Some rock stars never **learn** _______ or write music.
5 A lot of rock stars **decide** _______ in the USA, where they make more money and pay lower taxes.
6 Madonna played at a concert in my city last month. I **tried** _______ tickets but it was impossible. She's too popular.

## GRAMMAR 2 Complete the sentences so they are true for you.

1 I want to __________________________ before I'm 40.
2 Next year I plan to __________________________.
3 One day I hope to __________________________.
4 I learnt to __________________________ when I was __________________ ________ years old.

## SPEAKING Talk to a partner and answer the questions.

1 Do you buy records or CDs, or do you download music from the Net?
2 How do you think people will buy music in future?
3 Do you know *Gorillaz*? Do you like them?
4 If you don't know *Gorillaz*, would you like to hear them?

# Effective *Skills*

**ACTIVATING VOCABULARY**

**Tick (✓) the boxes to answer the questions. Use a dictionary to check the words in bold.**

| | | yes | no |
|---|---|---|---|
| 1 | Is there a lot of **reality TV** in your country? | ☐ | ☐ |
| 2 | Do you ever watch **talent shows?** | ☐ | ☐ |
| 3 | Can **viewers** phone in to **vote** on these shows? | ☐ | ☐ |

**Now use a dictionary and underline the correct words in each sentence.**

1 The person who chooses the winner of a talent show is *a judge / a lawyer / a referee.*

2 If a singer or musician needs to show other people their abilty, they go to *a gallery / an audition / a hearing.*

3 A game or competition that people try to win is sometimes called *a contest / a contrast / a contract.*

**SKIMMING AND SCANNING**

**Read the text and put the sentences into the correct spaces.**

1 *Popstars* was the first show of this type.

2 Not everyone is happy about these talent shows.

3 Reality talent shows like *Popstars, Pop Idol, Fame Academy,* and *X-Factor* are changing the pop music industry.

4 *Pop Idol* soon followed.

## Pop stars overnight

______________________________________________. All over the world the top ten is now full of singers who became famous after winning a talent show. *Pop Idol* is the most successful of these shows, and the makers of the programme have sold it to more than 30 countries around the world, from South America to Malaysia.

______________________________________________. Three judges went around New Zealand looking for singers to be in a pop group. Hundreds of young people came to the auditions, hoping to become famous. After weeks of fierce competition, the judges chose five of them to make up the group, which they called *TrueBliss*. Then the cameras followed the group as they learnt to sing and as they recorded their first song. The song went to number one in its first week.

__________________________________________. It started in Britain but was soon on all over the world. It was a talent contest to find the best new young singer in the country. Hundreds of young singers auditioned in front of the judges, who chose twelve to enter the final stage. During this final stage viewers could phone in and vote for the singer that they wanted to win the show. Thousands of people in each country phoned in to vote. The winner in Britain, Will Young, and the runner-up, Gareth Gates, became huge stars. In the USA, the winner of *American Idol*, Kelly Clarkson, quickly became a household name.

__________________________________________. Some people think that the singers and the music they make are artificial. They say that real musicians have to work hard to be successful, and that these shows make it more difficult for them. They think it is wrong that people who go on talent shows become famous overnight. But the shows are very popular and the winners go on to be very successful.

## READING FOR DETAIL

**Read the text again and put the events into the correct order.**

____ *Pop Idol* started.

____ *TrueBliss* had a number one record.

____ Will Young, Gareth Gates and Kelly Clarkson became famous.

____ A reality show started in New Zealand.

____ Five young singers became a pop group called *TrueBliss*.

## IDENTIFYING KEY WORDS

**Underline the correct word or phrase in each sentence and then write the key word in the space.**

**1** Competing to win *Popstars* was very **easy / difficult**.

The key word in line 9 is __________.

**2** Gareth Gates **was the winner / came second** on *Pop Idol*.

The key word in line 19 is __________.

**3** Some people don't like the music made by talent show winners because it's **not real / too loud**.

The key word in line 23 is __________.

**4** Talent show winners become famous **very quickly / quite slowly**.

The key word in line 26 is __________.

## LANGUAGE IN CONTEXT

**Read these lines again and match the extracts (1–6) to the definitions (a–f).**

1 **make up**, line 10
2 **the cameras followed**, lines 10 and 11
3 **went to number one**, line 12
4 **enter the final stage**, line 16
5 **huge stars**, line 20
6 **a household name**, line 21

**a** go into the last part
**b** everything was on film
**c** very famous people
**d** be part of
**e** a person that everyone knows
**f** was the best-selling record

## UNDERSTANDING PHRASAL VERBS

**Look at *make up* in line 10. If you know the verb part of a phrasal verb, you can understand the phrasal verb in context. Complete the sentences with these phrasal verbs, without using a dictionary.**

| grow up | save up | put up | look up | fill up |
|---|---|---|---|---|

1 When I'm reading, I often ____________ difficult words in a dictionary.
2 We haven't got much petrol. We need to stop and ____________ soon.
3 I need to ____________ £2,000 before I go to Australia next year.
4 A lot of little boys want to be football players when they ____________.
5 The first thing to do when you go camping is ____________ the tent.

## CORRECTING ERRORS

**Delete five unnecessary words in the notes. Then correct five spelling errors.**

*Talent shows are very populer in a lot of the different countrys. Pop Idol is the most famous. It started in Britain but is now shown all over in the world.*

*A lot of young singers are become sucessful after they win talent shows on TV. Kelly Clarkson won Pop Idol in the USA and is now a very famous. Some people they think that the music these singers make isn't as good as music that reel musicians make. They think it is arteficial.*

# 12 A healthy diet?

**PRE-READING 1** **Tick the correct definition for *junk food* in your dictionary.**

**A** food that is healthy and good for you

**B** food that is unhealthy and isn't very good for you

**Now put these types of food into the correct column.**

burgers sushi crisps fruit chips salad
fried noodles oily fish fresh vegetables sweets
fizzy drinks chocolate biscuits fruit juice

| healthy | unhealthy |
|---|---|
| __________ | __________ |
| __________ | __________ |
| __________ | __________ |
| __________ | __________ |
| __________ | __________ |
| __________ | __________ |
| __________ | __________ |

**PRE-READING 2** **Match the words and phrases in bold in the text to the definitions.**

1 someone whose job is to cook food __________
2 heavier than you should be __________
3 the place where people eat when they are at school or work __________
4 secretly taking things into or out of a place __________
5 the people who control a country __________
6 three substances that food can contain __________
7 to say that something is not allowed __________
8 occasions when you eat; for example, breakfast, lunch, and dinner __________

# No more junk food

**The government** in England wants to bring back healthy school lunches. It is going to **ban** chips, chocolate, and fizzy drinks from school **cafeterias**. There will be no more food that is high in ________________________.

It has made the decision after the popular TV **chef**, Jamie Oliver, made a programme about the poor quality of school **meals**. Millions of viewers were shocked to see children eat ________________________.

Starting next year, schools will have to make sure that their cafeterias regularly serve good-quality meat and oily fish. Children will get fresh vegetables or salad and fruit with every meal. From then on, burgers and sausages, potato and tortilla chips, chocolate and chocolate biscuits, sweets and ________________________ they will only occasionally be allowed to eat.

The government promises to spend about £240 million to improve school meals. A government official says, 'We want to provide children with a healthy meal that gives them the **protein, vitamins**, and **minerals** they need to learn and play. We also plan to help schools teach children about what makes a good diet, and how to prepare and cook healthy food. The number of **overweight** children in this country is much too high and we must do ________________________.'

Some schools are already serving the healthier options, but they are having a problem they didn't expect. Some older children are **smuggling** chocolate and packets of crisps into school to sell. Toby, a 16-year-old pupil in London, says, 'I can get almost £20 a day by selling stuff to younger kids in the playground.' It seems that it will not be so easy to make school children do ________________________.

**COMPREHENSION 1** **Read the text quickly and put the key phrases in the spaces at the end of each paragraph.**

chewing gum

salt and fat

what is good for them

so much junk food

something about it

## COMPREHENSION 2 Read the text again and answer the questions.

**1** In lines 4 and 5, *high in salt and fat* means …

**a** having a lot of salt and fat.
**b** having not much salt and fat.
**c** having no salt and fat.

**2** In line 7, *poor quality* means …

**a** something is good.
**b** something is bad.
**c** something is changing.

**3** In line 8, if you are *shocked to see* something, you …

**a** feel happy.
**b** are very surprised.
**c** are not interested.

**4** In line 9, *make sure* means …

**a** check that something is done.
**b** make something better.
**c** say that people can't do something.

**5** In line 14, if you *promise to* do something, you …

**a** say you will do it.
**b** try not to do it.
**c** can't do it.

**6** In line 22, *serving the healthier options* means that they are …

**a** offering better food.
**b** selling more burgers and chips.
**c** cooking bigger meals.

**7** In line 25, *a pupil* is …

**a** a child learning at school.
**b** a teacher at school.
**c** somebody who works in the cafeteria.

**8** In line 27, *stuff* means …

**a** books.
**b** pens and pencils.
**c** chocolate and crisps.

**9** In line 27, *the playground* is …

**a** inside the school building.
**b** outside the school building.
**c** part of the school cafeteria.

## COMPREHENSION 3

### Complete the sentences with some of the words in the box.

| diet | biscuits | cafeteria | meal | fizzy | oily |
|---|---|---|---|---|---|
| fresh | fat | chocolate | chef | junk | menu |

**1** I hope the _______________ is in English. I don't understand French.

**2** The _______________ who cooks in my favourite restaurant is quite famous.

**3** I usually have lunch in the _______________ at work, but I sometimes take sandwiches.

**4** There's a lot of _______________ on this meat. I don't think I can eat it.

**5** It's not good for children to have too many _______________ drinks.

**6** This bread isn't very _______________. When did you buy it?

**7** I can't eat cakes. I'm on a _______________.

**8** We went out for a lovely _______________ at the weekend.

### Now answer the questions about you. Compare your answers with a partner.

**1** Do you have a healthy diet?

**2** Do you eat a lot of junk food?

**3** Do you have your main meal of the day in the evening?

**4** Do you like fizzy drinks?

**5** Do you eat a lot of fresh fruit and vegetables?

**Grammar**

Present continuous

We use the present continuous to talk about actions that are in progress around the time we speak.

*Some* ***schools are*** *already* ***serving*** *the healthier options, but* ***they are having*** *a problem they didn't expect. Some older* ***children are smuggling*** *chocolate and packets of crisps into school.*

| | | |
|---|---|---|
| I | am | |
| you | are | |
| he / she / it | is | verb+ing |
| we | are | |
| they | are | |

## GRAMMAR 1 Complete the sentences with the verbs in the present continuous. Be careful about the spelling of the main verb.

The cafeteria at my school only served burgers and chips for a long time, but now everything (**1**)________________ (change). We can buy all sorts of salads and fresh fuit and vegetables. I think most of the kids (**2**)________________ (eat) more healthily than they did before.

I've always been quite a thin person, but now that I'm 30, I (**3**)________________ (put) on weight. My husband is also worried. He (**4**)________________ (get) quite fat, too. We (**5**)________________ (try) to do everything we can to stay healthy. I (**6**)________________ (drink) less wine, and my husband (**7**)________________ (do) more exercise. It isn't easy though. We (**8**)________________ both ________________ (miss) cakes and chocolate biscuits.

## SPEAKING Talk to a partner and answer the questions.

**1** Is there a cafeteria where you go to school?

**2** What kind of food do they serve? Is it healthy?

**3** Is it a good idea to make children eat more healthy food, or is it better for children to decide what they want to eat?

# Effective *Skills*

**PREDICTING / ACTIVATING VOCABULARY**

**You will read a text about people in the West changing to a Japanese diet. Here are some possible reasons. Tick (✔) the ones that you think will be in the text. Use a dictionary to check the words and phrases in bold.**

1 **Life expectancy** in Japan is very high. ☐
2 Japanese food doesn't have much **cholesterol**. ☐
3 Fewer people in Japan get **cancer**. ☐
4 People in Japan have lower **blood pressure**. ☐
5 People in the West want to eat with **chopsticks**. ☐
6 The Japanese eat a lot of nice **desserts**. ☐
7 Japanese people never suffer from **depression**. ☐
8 Japanese **ingredients** are becoming cheaper in the West. ☐

**SKIMMING AND SCANNING**

**Read the text quickly and tick (✔) the three sentences above that are definitely true.**

## Westerners turn to a Japanese diet

Many people in the West are turning to a 'Japanese diet'. Famous people like Victoria Beckham, wife of football star David Beckham, say that a diet of sushi and seaweed helps them to stay slim and healthy. Suddenly, all sorts of Japanese food products are available in the shops and a new book about dieting, *Japanese Women Don't Get Fat or Old*, is a best-seller.

Japan has the highest life expectancy in the world. Men live to an average age of 78, while many women live to 85. Some recent studies show that it might be because the Japanese eat a lot of soya and miso. Both are very low in cholesterol, and both contain substances that reduce the risk of cancer.

The Japanese also drink a lot of green tea, which doctors think may prevent cancer and reduce blood pressure. They eat smaller amounts of food at mealtimes and eat fewer desserts. Japanese people usually use chopsticks and so take longer over their meals. They give their body more time to digest food.

In Japan there is less stomach, breast, and kidney cancer. Older people in Japan seem to suffer from depression less than many older people in the West. Some doctors believe all this is because of the diet there.

Westerners think this is good news. In the past, they could only buy Japanese ingredients in specialist shops, but now they are on the shelves in many supermarkets and more and more people are asking for them.

## READING FOR DETAIL

**Tick (✔) the sentences True (T) or False (F).**

1 Victoria Beckham thinks that a Japanese diet helps her not to put on weight. T ☐ F ☐

2 It is difficult for people in the West to buy Japanese food products. T ☐ F ☐

3 A book about the Japanese diet is very popular. T ☐ F ☐

4 Japanese people live longer than people in the West. T ☐ F ☐

5 All Japanese men live to 78 years old. T ☐ F ☐

6 Japanese people eat very big meals. T ☐ F ☐

7 Japanese people eat their meals slowly. T ☐ F ☐

## UNDERSTANDING REFERENCES

**Underline the noun phrase that each pronoun refers to. In 5, write the noun into the space.**

1 In line 10, 'both' refers to *men and women / soya and miso*.

2 In line 13, 'They' refers to the *Japanese / doctors*.

3 In line 16, 'They' refers to *Japanese people / chopsticks*.

4 In line 19, 'this' refers to *there is less cancer and depression / everything about the Japanese diet*.

5 In line 19, 'there' refers to ______________________.

6 In line 22, 'them' refers to *Japanese ingredients / supermarkets*.

## VOCABULARY IN CONTEXT

**Complete the definitions with words and phrases from the text.**

**paragraph 1**

1 A green or brown plant that grows in the sea is ______________.

2 If you are thin in an attractive way, you are ______________.

3 If something is ______________ you can obtain it.

4 A book that many people buy is a ______________.

**paragraph 2**

**5** The ______________ of 20, 30, 40, and 50 is 35.

**6** The possibility that something bad may happen is the ______________.

**paragraph 3**

**7** When you change food in your stomach into substances that your body needs, you ______________ it.

**paragraph 4**

**8** A part of a female's body that produces milk is a ______________.

**9** A ______________ is one of two organs in your body that clean your blood.

**10** Another way to say that you have an illness is to say that you ______________ ______________ it.

**paragraph 5**

**11** If something is ______________ ______________ ______________,it is in the shops for people to buy.

**COMPLETING A TEXT**

**Delete words you don't need and write words in the spaces.**

*I think my diet is quite / very __________.*

*I eat a lot of ______________________________*

*and ______________________________.*

*I try not to eat too much /too many*

*______________________________.*

*For breakfast I usually ______________________________*

*and at lunchtime I ______________________________.*

*In the evening I ______________________________.*

*One thing I love is ______________________________*

*and one thing I never eat is ______________________.*

# Review Unit 11

## EXERCISE 1

**Read the text without a dictionary.**
**Write your starting and finishing time.**

Time started: ________

### Who needs a record label?

The British rock band, the *Arctic Monkeys*, has shown how the Internet is changing the music industry. They became famous (**1**)____________ the help of a major record label. The band (**2**)____________ their songs onto *MySpace*, where fans could download them for free. The fans made (**3**)____________ and passed them onto friends and (**4**)____________ everyone was talking about the *Arctic Monkeys*. When the band's first single, 'I Bet You Look Good on the Dancefloor' came out, it went (**5**)____________ to number one. Their first album, *Whatever People Say I Am, That's What I'm Not*, sold 360,000 copies in a week and was the (**6**)____________ selling album in history.

## EXERCISE 2

**Decide which of these word types go in each space. Write the letter in the space.**

**A** noun
**B** verb
**C** adjective
**D** adverb
**E** preposition

**Now choose the best option for each space from the list below.**

**1** under / without / for
**2** showed / delivered / posted
**3** copies / repeats / models
**4** later / secondly / soon
**5** straight / along / now
**6** longest / strongest / fastest

Time finished: ________

## EXERCISE 3

**Look at *came out* in line 8 of the text. Underline the correct meaning.**

**Came out** means *became available to buy / was written and recorded.*

**Now read these short extracts without a dictionary and underline the correct meaning.**

**1** Pop stars should behave in the right way. Children **look up to** them and often copy what they do.

**Look up to** means *to try to see them as often as possible / to respect them.*

**2** I was in a rock band when I was younger. When we played at our first concert, we expected a lot of people to come and see us. We were very disappointed when only ten people **turned up!**

**Turned up** means *arrived at the concert / were members of our band.*

**3** Music lessons at school were really boring. We just copied notes from the board. They **put** me **off** learning to play a musical instrument for a long time.

**Put** me **off** means *helped me to be interested / stopped me wanting to do something.*

**4** When I was little, I listened to pop music and bought a lot of singles. I soon **grew out of** that and started listening to classical music.

**Grow out of** means *stop doing something because you get older / start doing something new.*

# Review Unit 12

## EXERCISE 1

How quickly can you complete the survey? Read and check (✔) the option that is true for you in each question. Only use a dictionary if you don't understand a key word.

### Do you have a healthy diet?

1 **A** I try to eat something healthy for breakfast. ☐
**B** I don't usually have time to eat anything for breakfast. ☐

2 **A** I usually eat food that is boiled, baked, or grilled. ☐
**B** I usually eat food that is fried in oil. ☐

3 **A** I drink water during the day. ☐
**B** I drink coffee and/or fizzy drinks during the day. ☐

4 **A** I eat a lot of sweets and chocolate. ☐
**B** I don't eat a lot of sweets or chocolate. ☐

5 **A** I drink alcohol most nights of the week. ☐
**B** I don't drink alcohol / I drink very little alcohol. ☐

6 **A** I eat my main meal at lunchtime. ☐
**B** I often eat a big meal before I go to bed. ☐

## EXERCISE 2

Now look at the bottom of the page to see if you have a healthy diet.

## EXERCISE 3

Read each extract without a dictionary and underline the correct option.

1 It is very important to have a **balanced** diet. You need to eat meat, fish, vegetables, and fruit. You should try to eat rice, pasta, and potatoes if you can.

**Balanced** means *having a good mix of different things / having the same thing always.*

2 I always read the labels on the food I buy. I like to check that there aren't too many **additives** in it.

**Additives** are *natural substances in food / chemicals in food.*

3 I'm trying not to eat so many sweet things, but it's very difficult. When I see a cake or a chocolate bar, I just can't **resist** it.

**Resist** means *to stop yourself doing something that you would like to do / to have enough money to buy something.*

4 It isn't always a good idea to **peel** vegetables before you eat or cook them. Most of the goodness is in or just under the skin.

**Peel** means *to taste something before you eat it / to take the skin off something.*

5 Going out and having a few drinks is fine, but **binge drinking** is very dangerous. You are not in control of what you do and your body takes a long time to recover.

**Binge drinking** means *drinking too much alcohol in a short time / drinking something that is poisonous.*

**Survey results: Add up your score. 1:** A – 3 points / B – 0 points, **2:** A – 3 points / B – 0 points, **3:** A – 3 points / B – 0 points, **4:** A – 0 points / B – 2 points, **5:** A – 0 points / B – 3 points, **6:** A – 2 points / B – 0 points. *If you have ten points or more, you have a healthy diet!*

# Introduction

## About the author

William Sydney Porter was an American writer. He used the name **O. Henry**. He was born on 11 September 1862 in Greensboro, in the state of North Carolina. He did not have much education. He left school at the age of 15.

In 1882, Porter moved to the state of Texas. He worked on a ranch. Then he left the farm and from 1854 to 1886, he was a book-keeper in an office in Austin. He looked after the company's accounts.

William Porter married Athol Estes Roach in 1887. Athol and William had two children, a girl and a boy. Soon, William started writing articles and stories for magazines and newspapers.

Between 1891 and 1894, William worked at the First National Bank in Austin, Texas. In 1895, the police wanted to arrest him. He had taken money from the First National Bank. William ran away from the police and he went to Honduras. He stayed in Central America for a year.

But Athol was very ill and in 1897, William returned to America. Athol died that same year. After that, William was in prison for three years. In prison, he started writing short stories. Most of them were funny and they had unusual endings.

William Porter came out of prison in 1901. First, he lived in the state of Ohio. Then in 1902, he moved to New York City. William's second wife was Sara Lindsay Coleman. They got married in 1907. William earnt a lot of money, but he spent it all. He drank too much alcohol. William Porter died in a hospital in New York on 4 June 1910. He had only 23 cents in his pocket. He was 48 years old.

Some of William Porter's books are: *Cabbages and Kings* (1904), *The Four Million* (1906), *The Gentle Grafter* (1908) and *Options* (1909).

*A Good Burglar* and *The Jeweller's Wife* are taken from *The Last Leaf and Other Stories* by O. Henry, a title from the Macmillan Readers series.

## About these stories

O. Henry wrote stories about rich people and about poor people. Some stories are about criminals and detectives. At this time, criminals became more clever. Burglars broke into shops and people's houses. They stole money and property. Safe-crackers broke into banks. They used special tools and opened the banks' strong metal safes. They stole thousands of dollars.

More and more police detectives tried to stop the criminals. Each state had investigators – special policemen who worked for the government. They chased criminals and they investigated crimes. Private investigators worked for clients. The clients paid private investigators to find somebody or something.

# A Good Burglar

The place was North America. The year was 1900.

Jimmy Valentine was in prison. He was Prisoner Number 9762. Jimmy had been in prison for nine months. He wanted to get out of prison and his friends were trying to help him. His friends were talking to important people about him.

One day, Jimmy was making shoes in the prison workshop. A guard came into the room.

'The warden wants to talk to you, 9762,' the guard said. He took Jimmy to the warden's office.

'Valentine, you're a lucky man!' said the warden. 'You have powerful friends. The government has given you a pardon. Tomorrow, you'll be free. Listen to me, Valentine. You are not a bad young man. Don't come back to prison! You can change your life. You must live honestly now. You mustn't steal any more money. Stop burgling! Stop safe-cracking!'

'I'm not a safe-cracker, sir!' Jimmy said. 'I've never cracked a safe in my life!'

The warden laughed. 'Who cracked that safe in Springfield?' he asked. 'Didn't you do that job?'

'Springfield?' Jimmy replied. 'I've never been there in my life!'

'Take him away,' the warden said to the guard. 'Bring him here at seven o'clock tomorrow morning.'

Early the next morning, Jimmy was standing in the warden's office again. A prison clerk gave him a railroad ticket and five dollars. The warden shook Jimmy's hand. Then Prisoner Number 9762 became Mr James Valentine. He walked out of the prison, into the sunshine.

Outside the prison, the birds were singing. But Jimmy did not listen to them. He went to a restaurant and he had a good meal – a chicken and a bottle of wine. Then he got on a train.

Three hours later, Jimmy got off the train at a little town in Illinois. He went into a small bar and shook hands with the owner.

'Mike Dolan!' said Jimmy. 'How are you?'

'I'm sorry, Jimmy!' said Mike. 'We tried to get you out of prison sooner. But the Springfield police made trouble for us. Here's the key to your room.'

Mike gave him a key and Jimmy went upstairs to his room. He unlocked the door and he went inside. Nothing in the room had changed. Nobody had been inside it for nine months.

The police had arrested Jimmy in this room. Jimmy had fought them and one of Ben Price's shirt-buttons had come off in the fight. The great detective's button was still on the floor of the room.

My little friends!

Jimmy Valentine smiled. Then he pulled a dusty suitcase from behind the bed. He opened it carefully. Inside the case was the best set of burglar's tools in the United States. Jimmy had paid $900 for them! He had made some of the tools himself.

Half an hour later, Jimmy went downstairs again. He was wearing smart clothes and his suitcase was clean and bright.

'Are you going to do another job?' asked Mike.

'Me?' said Jimmy. 'A job? I don't understand you, Mike. I sell biscuits. I'm a salesman for the New York Cracker Company!'

Jimmy laughed. Mike laughed too.

One week later, there was a burglary in Richmond, Indiana. The burglar took $800 from an old safe. Two weeks after that, somebody stole $1500 from a new safe in Logansport, Indiana. Then $5000 disappeared from a safe in a bank in Jefferson City, Missouri.

Ben Price investigated these three burglaries.

'Jimmy Valentine is working again!' he said.

Ben Price knew all about Jimmy Valentine. Jimmy worked alone. And he travelled many miles between jobs. Jimmy moved fast. And he enjoyed good clothes, good food and fine wine.

'I'll catch him,' the detective said to himself. 'And next time, he'll stay in prison. Next time, there will be no government pardon for him.'

One afternoon, Jimmy and his suitcase arrived at the little town of Elmore. Elmore was in Arkansas. The town was five miles from the nearest railroad station.

Jimmy walked along Elmore's main street. He was young. He was handsome. He wore good clothes. Not many young men in Elmore were as good-looking as Jimmy Valentine.

A beautiful young lady walked along the street towards him. Jimmy Valentine looked into her eyes – and he fell in love. The young lady's cheeks became red. She passed him. Jimmy turned and watched her entering the Elmore Bank.

A boy was playing in the street outside the bank. Jimmy gave the boy a coin and asked him some questions about the town. After a few minutes, the young lady came out of the bank.

Jimmy gave the boy another coin. 'Who is that young lady?' he asked.

'She's Miss Annabel Adams,' replied the boy. 'Her father owns the bank.'

Jimmy walked to the Planters' Hotel and he asked for a room.

'My name is Ralph D. Spencer,' he told the hotel clerk. 'I want to start a business here. Is there a shoe shop in Elmore?'

'No, there isn't a shoe shop here,' the clerk replied. 'This town needs a shoe shop. You'll like Elmore, Mr Spencer. The people here are very friendly.'

'I'll stay for a few days,' said Jimmy. 'I'll look around the town.'

'Do you want someone to carry your suitcase up the stairs?' asked the clerk.

'No, I'll carry it myself,' Jimmy replied. 'It's very heavy.'

'Mr Ralph Spencer' stayed in Elmore. Soon, he owned a small shoe shop in the town. The shop was successful. People liked Mr Spencer and they respected him. He made many friends. And soon, he met Miss Annabel Adams.

At the end of the year, Ralph D. Spencer and Annabel Adams were engaged to be married.

Annabel loved Ralph Spencer and she was proud of him. And her father, the owner of the Elmore Bank, liked Ralph very much too. The Adams family often invited him to their home.

One day, two weeks before the wedding day, Jimmy was sitting in his room at the Planters' Hotel. He thought for a while, then he wrote a letter. It was a letter to a friend in St Louis, Missouri.

Planters' Hotel, Elmore

Tuesday

Dear Billy,

Please meet me at Sullivan's Bar in Little Rock, Arkansas, next Wednesday night. I want to give you my tools. I'm an honest man now. I've got a nice shoe shop in this town. And, in two weeks, I'm going to marry the best girl in the world. She believes in me. She trusts me and she is proud of me.

I'll never do another wrong thing. Please come to Sullivan's Bar. I'll bring the tools with me.

Your friend,

Jimmy Valentine

The next Monday, Ben Price arrived in Elmore. The detective talked to many people.

He asked them about Jimmy Valentine. Nobody in the town knew Jimmy Valentine. But everybody talked about Ralph D. Spencer.

Soon, Ben Price started to watch the owner of the shoe shop.

'Jimmy! You're going to marry the banker's daughter,' the detective said to himself. 'That's very interesting!'

On Tuesday morning, Jimmy had breakfast at the banker's house, outside the town.

'I'm going to Little Rock today,' he told the family. 'I want to buy my wedding-suit. And I want to buy something nice for Annabel.'

'I want you to see something at the bank first,' said Mr Adams.

After breakfast, they all walked into the town together – Mr Adams, Jimmy, Annabel and Annabel's sister with her two little girls. They stopped at the Planters' Hotel and Jimmy brought his suitcase from his room. Then they all walked on towards the bank.

Inside the bank, Jimmy put down his suitcase. Annabel tried to lift it. She laughed.

'Ralph, your case is very heavy!' she said.

'Yes, my dear,' Jimmy replied. 'There are lots of heavy shoes in it.'

Mr Adams took his family and Jimmy behind the high railings, into the banking-room.

Elmore Bank had a new strong-room. Mr Adams was very proud of it. He wanted to show the new strong-room to his family, and to his friend, Ralph Spencer.

'Some men from a company in Little Rock built it,' Mr Adams said. 'They finished it yesterday.'

The strong-room had a very thick steel door. There was a special lock on the door – a combination lock. The banker explained about the lock to his friend.

'This is a combination lock,' he said. 'There isn't a key. The numbers on those four knobs unlock the door. But we mustn't close the door. I haven't chosen the numbers for the combination.'

Everybody was interested in the strong-room. The two little girls, May and Agatha, loved the shiny metal door. They loved the big, shiny handle. And they loved the knobs with numbers on them.

Ben Price had seen the banker's family enter the bank with Jimmy. After a few minutes, the great detective followed them into the building.

Ben Price looked through the railings, into the banking-room.

'Good morning, sir,' one of the clerks said to him. 'Do you need some help?'

'No, thank you,' said the detective. 'I'm waiting for someone. I'm going to meet a friend here.'

Behind the railings, Annabel and her sister suddenly screamed. May, the sister's older child, had closed the door of the strong-room. Then she had turned all the knobs. But the other child, Agatha, was inside the strong-room!

Mr Adams ran to the steel door. He pulled the big handle.

'I can't open it!' he shouted. 'Nobody has chosen the numbers for the lock!'

'Oh, what shall we do?' Annabel's sister asked.

'There isn't much air in the strong-room,' Mr Adams said. 'I must send for a man from the lock company. But the company is in Little Rock!'

Agatha's mother screamed again. 'My darling will die!'

Mr Adams' face was white. 'Please be quiet, everybody,' he said. Then he shouted through the thick steel door.

'Agatha!' he shouted. 'Agatha! Listen to me. We'll get you out of there soon!'

The child was alone in the dark strong-room. She was only five years old and she was very frightened. The family heard her crying.

Jimmy put the rose in his coat pocket. Then he took off his coat and he pulled up the sleeves of his shirt. And suddenly, Ralph D. Spencer, the owner of the shoe shop, became Jimmy Valentine, the safe-cracker!

'Everybody must move away from the strong-room door,' he said.

Jimmy lifted his suitcase onto a table and opened it. Quickly and carefully, he took out the strange, shiny tools. He sang quietly to himself. Everybody watched him. Nobody spoke.

After a few minutes, one of Jimmy's special tools was cutting into the steel door. After ten minutes, he had cut out the locks. And one minute after that, Jimmy pulled the big handle and the door opened.

Little Agatha fell into her mother's arms. The child was frightened but she was not hurt.

Jimmy Valentine had cracked the strong-room door in less than fifteen minutes. It was the fastest job of his life.

Jimmy put on his coat. He walked through the banking-room, towards the street door. He heard a young woman's voice behind him.

'Ralph! Come back!'

But Jimmy did not turn round.

A big man was standing in front of the door. It was Ben Price.

'Hello, Ben!' said Jimmy. 'You've found me. I won't fight you this time. Arrest me. Take me away. I don't care any more.'

Ben Price looked past Jimmy. He looked at Annabel. He looked at the mother and her children in the banking-room. They were all crying quietly.

'You've made a mistake, Mr – Mr Spencer,' the detective said. 'I don't understand you.'

Then the great detective turned and walked out of the bank.

# The Jeweller's Wife

Mr Thomas Keeling wanted to be a private detective. Many people needed private detectives. Sometimes, a businessman wanted somebody to investigate his clerk. Was the clerk stealing his money? Sometimes, a lady wanted somebody to watch her husband. Was her husband meeting another woman? The businessman and the wife both needed a private detective. People needed Mr Thomas Keeling!

Mr Keeling was a quiet, serious man. He wanted to do his job well. He had read many books about famous detectives. He had saved $900. He was going to start a business.

One day, Mr Keeling came to Houston, Texas. He rented a small office in a quiet street. He put a sign outside his office and he waited for his first client.

For three days, Mr Keeling sat in his office and he read detective stories. But on the fourth day, a client came up the stairs to the office.

Mr Keeling looked at his client carefully. He saw a young lady. She was about twenty-five years old. She was tall and slim. Her black clothes were smart. She wore a black hat. A thin black veil covered her face.

'Good afternoon, madam,' said Mr Keeling. 'Please sit down.'

The lady lifted her veil.

Her face was lovely and she had large, grey eyes.

The lady spoke in a sad, soft voice.

'You are a stranger in this city, sir,' she said. 'That is the reason for my visit. I have a problem. I cannot speak about it to any of my friends. Mr Keeling, I want you to watch my husband.'

'Please tell me about your problem,' said Mr Keeling.

'My name is Mrs Robbins,' the lady said. 'My husband is a well-known man in this city. He has a small jewellry shop on Main Street. We have been married for five years. But my husband does not love me any more. He meets another woman secretly.'

Mr Keeling listened carefully. He said nothing.

'I want you to watch my husband,' Mrs Robbins said again. 'I want you to tell me about his movements. I will come to your office every second day. You will give me your reports. I will pay you well.'

She held out twenty dollars.

Mr Keeling took the money.

'I will help you, Mrs Robbins,' he said. 'Come here the day after tomorrow, at four o'clock. I'll give you my first report then. Good afternoon, dear lady.'

The detective began his investigation the next morning. He went to the jewellry shop on Main Street. He entered the shop and he looked around. The owner of the shop was working behind the counter.

The jeweller, Mr Robbins, was about thirty-five years old. His shop was small, but there were beautiful diamonds, expensive necklaces and fine watches on the shelves.

Later, the detective stood in the street near the jewellry shop for several hours. At last, something happened.

A young woman came along the street and she entered the shop. She had black hair and dark eyes. Her clothes were bright and colourful.

Mr Keeling went nearer to the shop and he looked through the window. The young woman walked up to the counter. She said something to Mr Robbins. He stopped working and the two of them talked quietly for a few minutes. Then the jeweller gave the woman some coins. A moment later, she came out of the shop and she walked quickly down the street.

At four o'clock the next afternoon, Mr Keeling's client came to his office.

'What did you find out about my husband?' she asked.

'I saw a woman go into the jewellry shop,' said Mr Keeling. 'Your husband gave her some money. She was a young, dark-eyed woman. Her hair was black and her clothes were colourful.'

'That's her!' said the lady. 'Charles is giving her money! That's terrible!'

The lady held a handkerchief over her eyes. She was crying.

'Mrs Robbins, what do you want me to do now?' asked the detective. 'Do you want me to continue this investigation?'

'I want to see my husband and this terrible woman together,' replied the lady. 'I also want witnesses – I want other people to see them together. Then I want to end our marriage – I want a divorce.'

She gave the detective ten dollars.

'I shall come for your second report the day after tomorrow,' she said. 'I'll come at four o'clock.'

Two days later, the lady came to the detective's office for the second report.

'Please sit down, Mrs Robbins. I have some news for you,' said Mr Keeling. 'I went into the jewellry shop again this afternoon. The young woman was already there. I heard her speaking to your husband.'

'My husband is a terrible man!' the detective's client said angrily. 'He lies to me about his work!'

'Mrs Robbins,' said Mr Keeling. 'Tonight, you must watch the meeting between your husband and this young woman. You must hide in the shop and you must listen to their words.'

'Yes! I'll do it!' said the lady. 'A policeman lives on this street. He is a kind man. He knows my family. Please find him. Tell him about my husband. He must come with you to the shop tonight. You and he will be my witnesses.'

'I'll speak to him,' said the detective. 'Please come here again at seven o'clock. Then we'll go to the shop together.'

Mrs Robbins left the office. Mr Keeling found the policeman's house and he knocked on the door.

The detective explained his plan. He asked the policeman for his help.

'Mrs Robbins wants to catch her husband with this woman,' he said. 'Tonight, Mrs Robbins is going to hide in the shop. She is going to listen to their words. And she wants you to be a witness. But we have a problem. First, she has to get into the shop.'

'I'll help the lady,' said the policeman. 'Let me think about your problem. Yes! I have the answer! There's a little room at the back of the shop. She must enter by that door. But the door between that room and the shop is always locked. You'll have to open it for her.'

At seven o'clock that evening, the detective's client came to his office for the fourth time. Again, she was wearing black clothes and there was a veil over her face. After a few minutes, they went out onto the street together.

Mr Keeling and the lady walked slowly along the pavement. They stopped opposite the jewellry shop. They waited. At about eight o'clock, a young woman entered the shop. After a few minutes, she came out again with Mr Robbins. She was holding his arm. They walked away, down the street.

The lady in black began to cry quietly.

'Look at them!' she said. 'My terrible husband and that bad young woman!'

Mr Keeling took his client to the back yard of the shop. The lady opened a door in the wall and they entered the small room behind the shop.

The detective and his client crossed the room to a locked door.

'This is the door into the shop,' said the lady.

'Where are you going to hide?' the detective asked.

'I want to hide in the shop,' the lady replied. 'In the shop, there is a large table. A cloth covers the table, and it hangs down to the floor. I'll hide under the table. I'll listen to my husband and that woman. I'll hear every word. But how can I get into the shop? This door is locked.'

Mr Keeling took some special keys from his pocket. He tried to open the door with them. He put one key after another into the lock. At last, one of the keys unlocked the door. The lady went into the shop. Mr Keeling did not follow her.

'I'll lock the door from this side,' the lady told the detective. 'Give me your key. You must go now. Find my husband and that woman. Then get the policeman and follow them back to the shop. I'll listen to my husband and that woman from under the table. Then I'll come out from under the table. I'll open the street door. You and the policeman will come into the shop. You will both be my witnesses.'

Mr Keeling soon found the jeweller and the young woman. They were eating in a quiet restaurant. He waited in the street. After a few minutes, Mr Robbins and the young woman left the restaurant.

The detective went quickly to the policeman's house. Then the two men hurried to the jewellry shop. They looked through the window. The policeman was surprised. He spoke to Mr Keeling.

'I don't understand,' said the policeman. 'You told me, "Robbins took a young woman to a restaurant." Where is she?'

'*There she is*!' said Mr Keeling. He pointed through the window.

'Do you know the lady with Robbins?' asked the policeman.

'That's his secret friend,' said Mr Keeling.

'No! You're wrong! That's Robbins' wife,' said the policeman. 'I've known her for fifteen years.'

'*What?*' the detective shouted. His face became pale. 'Who is under the table in the shop?'

He started to kick the door of the jewellry shop.

Mr Robbins came to the door and opened it. The policeman and the detective ran into the shop.

'Look under that table!' shouted the detective. 'Look under the cloth. Be quick!'

The policeman lifted the cloth and put his arm under the table. He pulled out a black dress, a black veil and a woman's wig.

'Is this young lady your wife?' Mr Keeling asked the jeweller. He pointed at the woman.

'Yes! She is my wife!' said Mr Robbins angrily. 'Why did you kick my door? Why are those clothes under my table?'

'Please check all the jewellry in your shop, Mr Robbins,' the policeman said. 'Is anything missing?'

Some diamond rings and some expensive necklaces were missing. Some watches were missing too. The missing jewellry was worth $800.

Later that night, Mr Keeling was sitting in his office. He was looking through a big book of photographs. They were photographs of criminals. The policeman had brought the book to the detective's office. Suddenly, Mr Keeling stopped turning the pages. He looked at a picture of a good-looking young man with a smooth face. He read the words underneath the photograph.

JAMES H. MIGGLES, also known as 'The Unhappy Wife'.

Description: Tall and slim. Grey eyes.

Crime: Burglary.

Miggles usually wears women's clothes. He is clever and dangerous. The police in Kansas City, New Orleans and Chicago are searching for him.

The next morning, Mr Keeling paid the jeweller $800, then he closed his office.

Mr Thomas Keeling, private detective, does not work in Houston any more.